Praise for Coffee w

"Like the first cup of the day, Coffee with Jesus offers a much-needed jolt to our culturally captured versions of Christianity and some beloved sacred cows. Yup—including my own."

SEAN GLADDING, author of *The Story of God, The Story of Us* and *Ten*

No cows were harmed in the making of this comic strip.

"Coffee with Jesus is one of my guilty pleasures. I read its sassy Jesus as a refuge from sober Christians and to make up for the smart-aleck gene missing from my DNA."

DAVID NEFF, former editor in chief, *Christianity Today*

"Sassy" seems a bit strong.

"Sometimes I wonder if one of Jesus' love languages is 'hang out'—you know, time together, minus the quality part. In this little collection of pithy, advice-columnesque comic strips, David Wilkie nails this little love language of Jesus. It might be going too far to call these little comic strips modern icons, but they do serve that purpose."

CHRIS HEUERTZ, author of *Unexpected Gifts: Discovering the Way of Community*

Yeah, that'd be going too far, Chris.

"It's a comic strip, so it's funny, right? Yes, of course. But it's also poignant, and pointed. And rife with good theology. So read it for a laugh, but be prepared to be challenged as well. Jesus probably has something to say to you too."

TONY JONES, blogger and theologian

So earnest, Tony. You're kinda takin' the fun out of this.

"I remember when the 'What Would Jesus Do?' tsunami almost completely engulfed all of us who worked with teenagers. Suddenly, we felt compelled to provide an answer to that impossible question. Problem was: most of us didn't have a clue what Jesus would do, really. And any honest reading of the Gospels reveals that his disciples didn't know what Jesus would do either. Coffee with Jesus steps into that same tension, responding with plucky, snarky and occasionally awkward honesty. We don't really know the full answer to 'What Would Jesus Say?' But I'd sure like it to be close to the Jesus in these panels."

MARK OESTREICHER, partner, The Youth Cartel

Radio Free Babylon Presents . . .

Coffee
with
Jesus

David
Wilkie

IVP Books

An imprint of InterVarsity Press
Downers Grove, Illinois

InterVarsity Press
P.O. Box 1400, Downers Grove, IL 60515-1426
World Wide Web: www.ivpress.com
Email: email@ivpress.com

InterVarsity Press® is the book-publishing division of InterVarsity Christian Fellowship/USA®, a movement of students and faculty active on campus at hundreds of universities, colleges and schools of nursing in the United States of America, and a member movement of the International Fellowship of Evangelical Students. For information about local and regional activities, write Public Relations Dept., InterVarsity Christian Fellowship/USA, 6400 Schroeder Rd., P.O. Box 7895, Madison, WI 53707-7895, or visit the IVCF website at www.intervarsity.org.

Design: Cindy Kiple
Images: Public domain

ISBN 978-0-8308-3662-8 (print)
ISBN 978-0-8308-8410-0 (digital)

Printed in the United States of America ∞

Library of Congress Cataloging-in-Publication Data

Wilkie, David J., 1963-
  Coffee with Jesus / David J. Wilkie.
     pages cm
  Includes bibliographical references.
  ISBN 978-0-8308-3662-8 (pbk. : alk. paper)
1. Jesus Christ—Comic books, strips, etc. 2. Christian life—Comic
books, strips, etc. I. Title.
  BT205.W47 2013
232.02'07—dc23

                                                 2013032475

P	25	24	23	22	21	20	19	18	17	16	15	14	13	12	11	10	9	8	7	6	5	4	3	2
Y	34	33	32	31	30	29	28	27	26	25	24	23	22	21	20	19	18	17	16	15	14	13		

For Karen Kay.
You're a saint.

Contents

Acknowledgments

Effusive thanks to the following people, without whose encouragement and help this book would not have been realized.

Joy and Kylah: the very first supporters of Radio Free Babylon, as if they had a choice.

My Springfield brothers: Jim Cox, Dave Cron, Bill Elliott, Brett Piper, Dan Spadoni and Josh Wellborn, who didn't bail, even though they were pretty sure I was insane.

My editor at InterVarsity Press, Dave Zimmerman, who took a chance, rolled the dice, and knew all along that it wasn't a gamble at all, and then organized, compiled and made some sense of this collection.

Laura Zderad, artist extraordinaire, for her patience in dealing with a guy with caveman-like Photoshop skills, and her colleagues in longsuffering, Cindy Kiple and Beth Hagenberg.

To all the artists, writers, musicians, influences, family and friends, both real and virtual, who've in varying ways been an encouragement: Fred Leo, Kym Davis, Richard Dresselhaus, Bill Green, Jason Fox, Wyatt Roberts, John Sanchez, Mark Duffy, Natasha Vargas-Cooper, Sara Champion, Stephen Wesley, Lorenz Schilling, Earl Creps, Jay and Donna Hostetler, Joe and Irene Batluck, Bob Knorpp, Darryl Ohrt, Emma Asante, Tony Wright, Howie Goldfarb, Josh Oakhurst, the 4th of July Kids, Sherry Nelson and Tony Shelley, John Shelton, Paula Zargaj-Reynolds, Steve Taylor, Phil Keaggy, John Michael Talbot, the Ward family, Greg Austin, Jim Harriger, Sam Knox, Bill and Kyle Neidt, Alistair Begg, Jim Wunderle, the coffee house gang from Gießen, Aaron Sprinkle, Dana, Cheri, Pam and Joy and our great parents, Dave and Jan, Lenette Hall, Mark and Cindy Simerly, Chester and Pam Strobel, Lucy Williams, Craig Olinger, Betsy Atkins, and Mitchell, Laura and Justin Fehlberg.

Very special thanks to the thousands of online friends I will never meet, for sharing, liking and commenting, and encouraging me with their love—as well as their hate.

And of course I owe buckets of thanks to my wife, Katie, who daily comes to my computer after I send her an instant message that says, "approval." She arrives hoping to laugh and often leaves saying, "Not funny," "You can do better," or "Uggghhh!" Rare is the day when she laughs out loud at a first draft, and many are the days when she isn't even smiling after five drafts. Without her I'd have published reams of my patented fourth-grade, stupid humor—or worse, humorless, sappy moralizing, as I tried to play to the factions in the crowd.

Finally, to Justin Charles and Luke Thomas, who reported from Texas that *Coffee with Jesus* was "pretty cool" and catching on in the local high school, just when I was about to throw in the towel, convinced that it had run its course.

Introduction

Coffee with Jesus was born out of my frustration with the heated political climate in my country. The ownership of the "Christian" thing to do, or the "Christian" way to vote, was being claimed by people and politicians from both ends of the political spectrum.

Coffee with Jesus was originally created as a one-off, single-panel comic on my blog. Utilizing old advertising clip art for the main characters and Sunday school clip art for the person of Jesus, I simply enjoyed the notion of Jesus appearing at table with these people (dressed as they were and sharing coffee with them) to refute their claims of how he might vote on any particular issue, to convince them that they cannot confuse their flag with their God—to set them straight, as it were. The notion of Jesus sitting down for a cup of coffee with a bunch of very certain and opinionated people struck me as humorous, and it did some others as well.

Soon, the Jesus of Coffee with Jesus was advising the recurring characters on their personal lives, their relationships, jobs, successes, failures, wants and needs. As a Christian, I wanted to show people a practical savior, one who used humor, sarcasm and gentle ribbing to address their concerns. Through various social media, the comic took off, and I soon felt the need and obligation to portray Jesus as I know him. "Those whom I love, I reprove and discipline" (Revelation 3:19 NASB) is a verse that came to mind whenever I had Jesus speaking a stinging rebuke, but it was time to show that he is, above all, merciful. Does he care about your first-world problems while other believers are being martyred in the third world? Yes, but he might put your problems in perspective for you. He's going to question your motives, examine your heart and reveal to you some ugly things you might be overlooking, all while loving you.*

---

*"How dare you put words in the mouth of Jesus that he never spoke!" was an often expressed concern. In fairness to those people, some of the early comics were just trying to be funny, where I'd go for the cheap punch line; any "truth" in the strip was fairly veiled. But far more people were expressing their appreciation for presenting the Jesus they

The concept of "Jesus the man" is something we've depicted in art for years. Who doesn't love the innocence (and even silliness) of those old Sunday school illustrations of Jesus walking through a field of flowers with a group of red, yellow, black and white children, a dog and a cat? ("And a happy little bird right over here, in this tree. Now, there's a happy bird!" said Bob Ross.) Or the beautiful depiction by Antonio Ciseri called *Ecce Homo*, where Jesus stands on the balcony before the mob as Pilate asks for the verdict? And with every question Pilate puts to him, Jesus answers him with another question, or he affirms what Pilate has spoken, or he simply doesn't reply at all. These are the actions of a revolutionary. This is a guy people followed. Not just because he could turn water into wine or feed a bunch of people with a little food or even heal their illnesses, but because he spoke truth, sometimes harshly, right into their souls. Even Pilate wanted to follow him, I think. But, being a politician . . .

While growing up, my notion of Jesus had always been of the sad and count-the-ribs skinny figure hanging at the front of the church, or of the sober, almost pudgy white guy peeling back his robes to reveal a flaming heart wrapped in thorns. And while he is the suffering savior, he is also the Jesus of the last book of the Bible, his hair white, a gold sash around his chest, his feet like bronze, his eyes a flaming fire! He can speak to me harshly, he can correct me; he can show me when I'm being an idiot and laugh with me when I finally see it, too.

Prayer is at the heart of *Coffee with Jesus*. The characters Carl, Lisa, Ann, Kevin and Joe are  in conversation with their God. His replies are the still, small voice—the whispers, the acknowledgments or pricks of conscience we get when we are quiet and waiting. The characters of *Coffee with Jesus* are often selfish and childish, bitter, angry, petty and jealous. They're comic characters after all, but a little of me is in all of them. They bring Jesus stupid requests that are far outside his will for them, like I sometimes do. And Jesus is usually patient with them. And he sometimes just wants to smack them upside the head and say, "What're you *thinking*?"

But he's always there. He always calls them by name, and his image in the two panels in which he appears in each episode never changes, underscoring that neither does he. And the characters do grow, but not too quickly, lest I run out of material. Perfect Christians are pretty annoying and not very funny at all.

While these comics have generated plenty of healthy debate, even ugly arguing, on the web, they've also been a unifier. They are shared by churches and people of every imaginable denomination and often by people of no denomination or faith at all. Baptists and Catholics, Brethren and Pentecostal, Lutherans, Presbyterians, Methodists, Episcopalians—dare I say, even Mormons—have identified enough with some of the comics within this book that they've shared them on their church websites, in their church bulletins or used them as sermon illus-

---

knew or had wanted to see, many of them outcasts from the church, not "churched" at all, agnostics and atheists.

trations. To me, that's worth any trouble creating this strip has been.

It fits a lyric I wrote sometime back to try to explain "Who are you guys?" when people would ask. *Unity* used to be a scary word in some Christian circles. I hope and believe that that time is passing.

ROOM IN THE BOAT

We're reformed.
We're fundamental.
We're traditional.
Experiential.
We're Shakers.
We're Quakers.
We're Baptists.
We're Trappists.
We're Friends.
We're with the Brethren.
We're addicts.
We're reverends.

We're insecure.
We're not so sure.
We're being cured.
We're not so pure.

We're Charismatic.
We're problematic.
We're Latter Rain.
We feel your pain.

We're old fashioned.
We're progressive.
We're laid back.
We're aggressive.
We're a throwback to the fast track.
We're with the Jew—and He's with you.
We're disciples.
We're students.
We're careless—and imprudent.

We're sinners. We're winners. The air
 seems thinner. We're at the dinner.

Where you've been and where you're
 gonna be
is not for us to see.
What you did and what you're gonna do
is not what qualifies you.
Is it true that we're just what we
 perceive—
or what we think we believe?
We're just trying to finish the float—
 and there's room in the boat.

1

Come See a Man

Getting to Know Jesus

She'd been married five times, and was living with a new guy; just minding her own business, she was grabbing some water at the well on the edge of town, perhaps in preparation for the evening meal or to do some cleaning. Maybe she had a few kids, some of them with different last names. Perhaps her new man was a total loser, bad stepdad, heavy drinker. Who knows? We can safely assume that anyone married five times and living with someone new is probably on a perpetual search for something better. This Samaritan woman knew enough about Jewish theology to have heard that a Messiah was coming, and she expressed hope in that to the Jewish man who boldly asked her for a cup of water. She was a seeker.

He revealed himself to her with a simple, "I'm the Messiah you're talking about." She rushed into town, and somehow the townspeople followed her back out to the well. Something must've been obvious. This was, after all, Ms. Get Her Water at Midday So as to Avoid the Clucking Old Hens Who Look Down on Her. She was clearly excited. "Come see a man who told me everything I ever did! Could this be the Messiah?"

So, she's not yet a believer. Even though he already told her he was the Messiah, she's still wondering, "Could this be?"

Jesus stayed in town for two days. I can see some guys leaning in doorways, just within earshot of where Jesus was doing his teaching. They probably said, "Nice guy. Good words, excellent teacher." Another one: "I never met a cooler Jew. Usually those guys don't even talk to us. This one seems pretty down-to-earth."

"Could this be the Messiah?" would be asked again over drinks in the town's taverns, out in the fields among some farm families—even back at the well, where the woman who first met him was perhaps now welcome to get her water in the mornings with the other women.

"Many of the Samaritans from that town believed in him because of the woman's testimony." And then, "And because of his words many more became believers."

Many. And then many more. Not all. A two-day seminar with the man himself, telling them who he is, how to worship God, how to find peace, and there were still some in the town who found other answers for the question of, "Could this be?"

Dead Serious

Back then, in Bible times, did you have a sense of humor, Jesus?

Nope. Walked around dead serious, somber. Once in a while I could muster a weak smile when kids came up to me. Or puppies.

Bummer. I'd always thought you were fully human as well as being fully God. ...*Wait.* You're playing with me, aren't you, J-Man?

Gotcha, Carl!

So, a Catholic and a Baptist walk into a bar—stop me if you've heard this one.

Reverence and Awe

I don't get why we're supposed to fear you, Jesus. I'm not *afraid* of you.

Not fear like a dog hiding under the bed during a noisy thunderstorm, Ann.

So, like reverence and awe then, like a professor who has the power to pass or fail you.

Yeah, that's close, but maybe the dean of admissions is a better analogy.

About to Say

Do you know what I'm about to say, Jesus; what I want to ask of you?

Of course, Lisa.

That must get boring for you.

Not at all. Love your company.

And after a while, you'll have a pretty good idea of what I'm about to say, too.

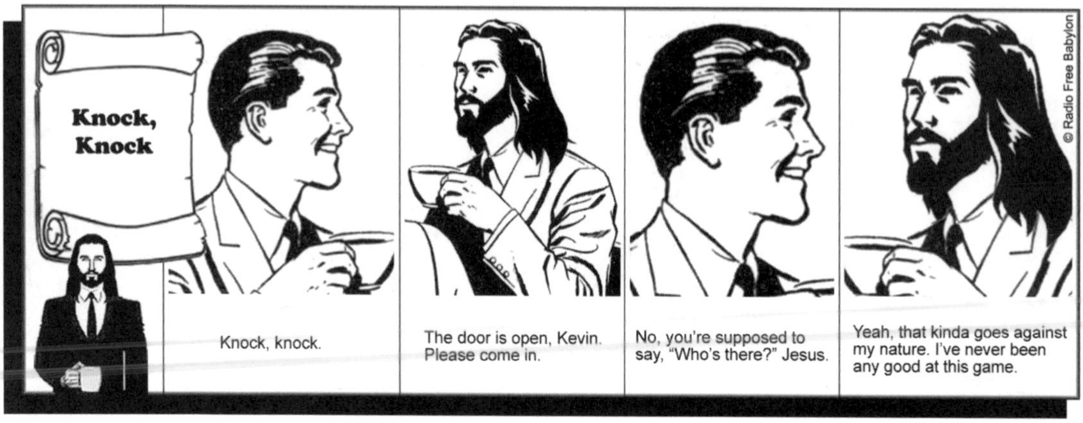
Knock, Knock
Knock, knock.
The door is open, Kevin. Please come in.
No, you're supposed to say, "Who's there?" Jesus.
Yeah, that kinda goes against my nature. I've never been any good at this game.
© Radio Free Babylon

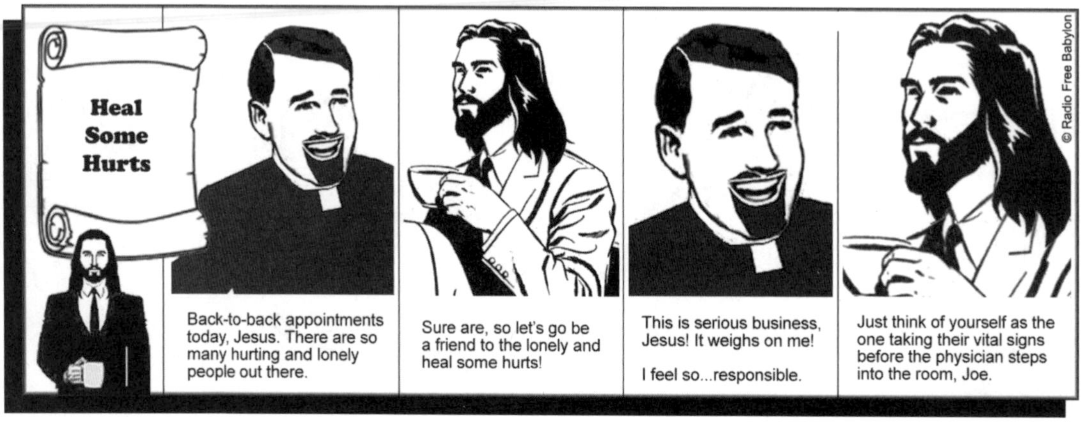
Heal Some Hurts
Back-to-back appointments today, Jesus. There are so many hurting and lonely people out there.
Sure are, so let's go be a friend to the lonely and heal some hurts!
This is serious business, Jesus! It weighs on me!
I feel so...responsible.
Just think of yourself as the one taking their vital signs before the physician steps into the room, Joe.
© Radio Free Babylon

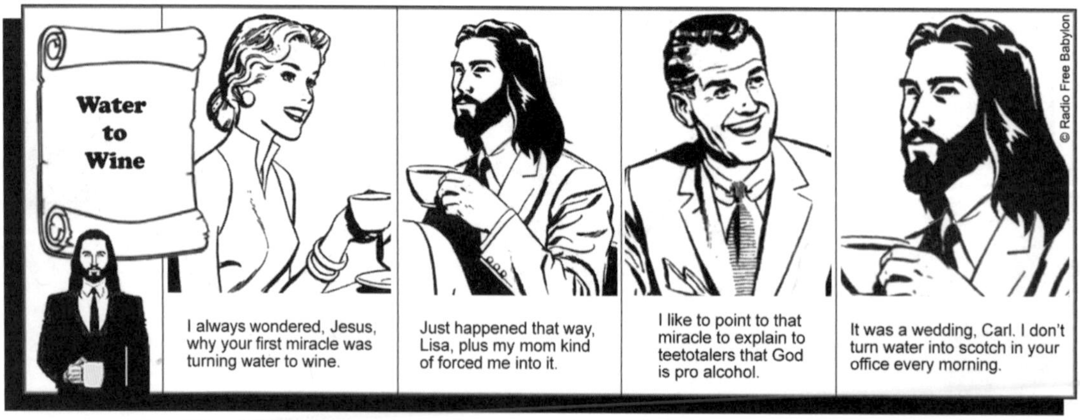
Water to Wine
I always wondered, Jesus, why your first miracle was turning water to wine.
Just happened that way, Lisa, plus my mom kind of forced me into it.
I like to point to that miracle to explain to teetotalers that God is pro alcohol.
It was a wedding, Carl. I don't turn water into scotch in your office every morning.
© Radio Free Babylon

Hide and Seek

What did kids do for fun back in your time, Jesus? I know my own kids would probably *die* if they didn't have Xbox, TV, smart phones and all that.

When we were allowed to play, which wasn't very often, we'd play your basic childhood games like Tag or Hide and Seek.

That must've been unfair to the other children. I mean, because you could always find them or never be found if you chose, right?

I didn't cheat, Ann. Contrary to what you may have read in some fanciful old "lost books," I wasn't known as "The Magic Boy of Nazareth."

Righteous

I wanna be a *righteous* man, Jesus.

When you stand before a holy God, Kevin, what could possibly make you "righteous" in his eyes?

Uhhhh...

...you?

There ya go.

Don't forget it.

A Little Privacy

Sometimes I could use a little privacy, Jesus. I mean, do you have to ALWAYS be there?

Even unto the end of the age, Carl.

That's disturbing.

Only when you're trying to hide.

Trash Talk

You're messin' with the wrong crew, Son of Man! I told you: this is *my* turf. I can see I'm gonna have to teach you a lesson.

Who do you think you're scaring, Satan? I will stomp you like a low-life snake.

You and me, boy king! Valley of Megiddo! End of Days! BE there!

You'd better pack a lunch.

Judge Not

"Judge not lest ye be judged" is my motto, Jesus. Too many of your people forget that verse.

And too many people who aren't mine take that verse out of context to judge those who are, Kevin.

Well, we're just pointing out to your judgmental people that they aren't living by your words.

I appreciate the help, Kevin, but I'll be the judge of that.

Falling Stars

Our society is so quick to turn on a celebrity. As soon as someone gets a little too big, then we all want to take them down.

It's always been that way, Ann. People love rising stars, but they delight in falling stars even more.

I guess you would know. Hailed as a king on your way into Jerusalem, then they're shouting, "Kill him!" a week later.

There was a very rapid change in the public mood, for sure. Ugly scene.

But you know, I'd do it again.

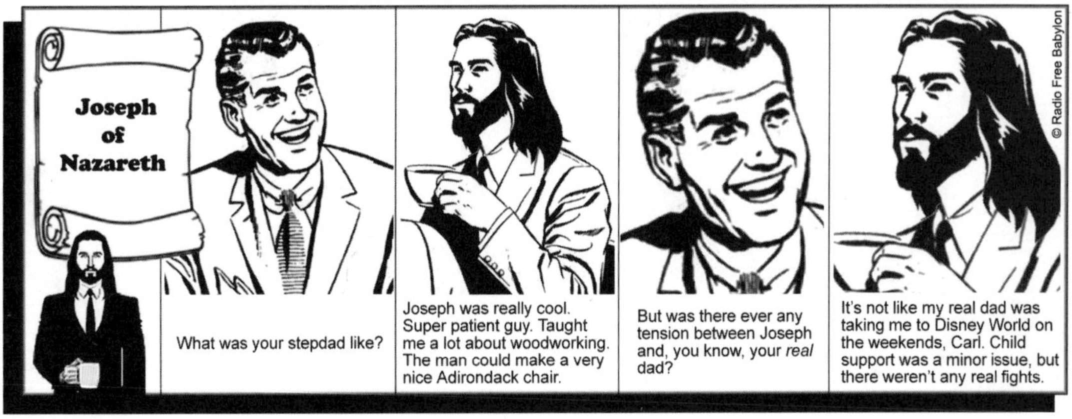
Joseph of Nazareth
What was your stepdad like?
Joseph was really cool. Super patient guy. Taught me a lot about woodworking. The man could make a very nice Adirondack chair.
But was there ever any tension between Joseph and, you know, your *real* dad?
It's not like my real dad was taking me to Disney World on the weekends, Carl. Child support was a minor issue, but there weren't any real fights.
© Radio Free Babylon

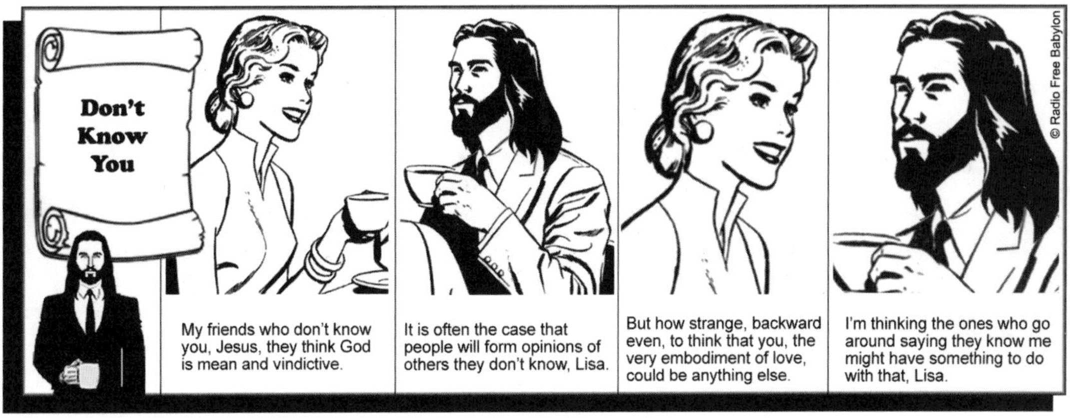
Don't Know You
My friends who don't know you, Jesus, they think God is mean and vindictive.
It is often the case that people will form opinions of others they don't know, Lisa.
But how strange, backward even, to think that you, the very embodiment of love, could be anything else.
I'm thinking the ones who go around saying they know me might have something to do with that, Lisa.
© Radio Free Babylon

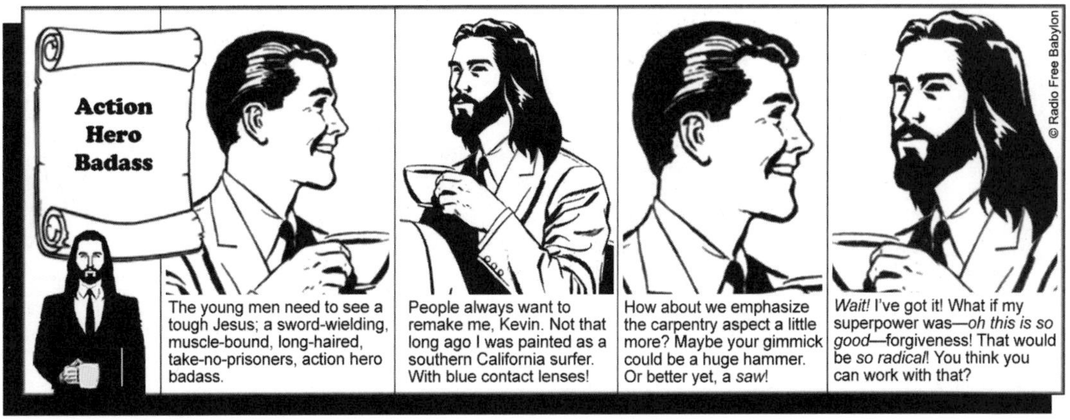
Action Hero Badass
The young men need to see a tough Jesus; a sword-wielding, muscle-bound, long-haired, take-no-prisoners, action hero badass.
People always want to remake me, Kevin. Not that long ago I was painted as a southern California surfer. With blue contact lenses!
How about we emphasize the carpentry aspect a little more? Maybe your gimmick could be a huge hammer. Or better yet, a *saw*!
Wait! I've got it! What if my superpower was—*oh this is so good*—forgiveness! That would be *so radical*! You think you can work with that?
© Radio Free Babylon

Did He Really?

And the flames of *hell*, Kevin, shall lick at your body *forever*! And I will be there with you, to ensure your *eternal torment*!

No, that's not possible!

Jesus redeemed me!

Hahaha! Oh, did he now?

Did he *really*, Kevin?

Kevin! Over here, son!

And yeah, really.

Tongues

How do you keep all of it straight, Jesus? I mean, there must be fifty million prayers coming at you every second in a hundred languages!

κομμάτι του κέικ

muito fácil para mim

相当简单

Whoa! Don't go speaking in tongues on me, Jesus!

That stuff freaks me out.

No need for alarm, Carl. Three other people in Greece, Brazil and China simultaneously asked me the same thing. I basically said, "Piece of cake."

Pretty Much Nothing

My boyfriend wants to "take a break," my landlord raised the rent and my cat ran away.

Nothing *lasts*, Jesus!

Yeah, Ann.

Pretty much nothing.

I come to you with my burdens and all you can say is, *"Yeah, duh! You're right, Ann! Nothing lasts!"*?

I said, "pretty much," Ann.

Myself excluded.

The Original
COFFEE WITH JESUS

Not That Jesus

I find it odd, Jesus, that nowhere in the entire Bible do we have a description of your physical appearance.

Yeah! We're left picturing you in our heads based on years of artwork.

Half of which was clearly created by the devil to make you look like a total wuss.

You'll find a description of my appearance in the last book of the Bible.

No, not the scary, white-haired guy with a sword coming out of his mouth, bronze feet and fiery eyes. That's Future Jesus.

Yeah, not that Jesus, Jesus.

The white-robed nice guy, long hair shining in the sun, straight, white teeth, maybe a little buff from all that carpentry work.

Throwing my head back in laughter? With blue eyes and a beautiful tan, Lisa?

Just tell me you weren't a red-headed, pasty-skinned, sad-faced wimp with a weak, scraggly beard.

Or the hunky dreamboat of Lisa's fantasy.

Cupcake or beefcake, it doesn't matter...

You'll know me when you see me.

What Would Jesus Eat?

Some friends of mine were saying that you were a member of the Essene sect, Jesus, and that you were a vegan.

I'm pretty much a fish connoisseur, Ann. As for the Essenes, people will say I am all sorts of things to support their own beliefs.

So true. I also heard some gay guys saying that you and your disciple John were like...you know.

You know me, just your average gay, vegan, pro-gun, anti-tax, military hawk with a pacifist streak.

Trek Through Asia

I've heard that in your teen years, maybe your twenties, you went on a lengthy journey to study with the great eastern mystics. Is that true?

We were blue collar, Kevin. We worked six days a week, went to synagogue on the seventh. I didn't have time for a trek through Asia.

I guess that explains why we don't know much about your life from the age of twelve until you started your ministry. It was *boring.*

It would make for monotonous reading, that's true. *"After making some chairs, they took their noon meal. Then they made some more chairs."*

Life Is Improv

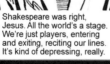

Shakespeare was right, Jesus. All the world's a stage. We're just players, entering and exiting, reciting our lines. It's kind of depressing, really.

The play has an outline, this is true, Carl, but there's no script. Life is improv. It's *exciting!* We act, react, and the play moves along.

But you know what I"m about to say! What I'm going to do tomorrow! Where I'll be in five years! When I'm going to die!

So *what?*
You don't!

That, my friend, should excite you!

Déjà Vu

The routine of life. Every day the same. I feel like I'm living in a permanent state of *déjà vu*, Jesus.

Be thankful for predictability, Ann. But really, today is all there is. Yesterday's gone, tomorrow's not here, etcetera, etcetera—you know the drill.

It's happening again! Right now! I feel like we've talked about this before—just like this!

We have, Ann, many times—hence the "etcetera, etcetera." Kinda hoping one of these days the concept is going to stick.

Soon

When are you returning, Jesus?

Soon, Kevin.

Yeah, you said that two thousand years ago.

Remember when you were a kid, Kevin, and Christmas break was like an eternity? For me, two thousand years is like, whatever.

I'm There

Some days, Jesus, you feel so far away. It's like I'm not getting through to you.

Don't trust your feelings, Carl.

So you're there? Always?

Even when you feel like shouting, "My God, my God, why have you forsaken me?" I'm there, Carl.

© Radio Free Babylon

So Wimpy

It's always puzzled me, Jesus, how a carpenter followed by fishermen, drunkards and whores could be portrayed as so—sorry about this—*wimpy*.

Have you ever read an email or a text, Lisa, and ascribed to the sender a tone they didn't intend?

Oh, sure. Happens all the time. It's so easy to read the wrong intention or even inflection into the written word.

Well, Lisa, I was popular for a reason, and it wasn't for my timid, shy personality.

Read between the lines.

Buried or Cremated

Some of my people have asked me, Jesus, should they be buried or cremated?

A lot of bodies have been vaporized, burned or have just disintegrated over time, Joe.

So, come the resurrection of the dead...

I'll be resurrecting the dead, Joe.

It won't be an issue.

Shroud of Turin

So, Jesus...Shroud of Turin...

Is it really your burial cloth?

If I answer, "Yes," is your faith strengthened, Kevin? Or if I answer, "No," is your faith weakened?

It was a simple "yes" or "no" question, Jesus. I don't know why you have to get all philosophical on me.

OK. Let me rephrase my answer in simpler terms:

What's it matter?

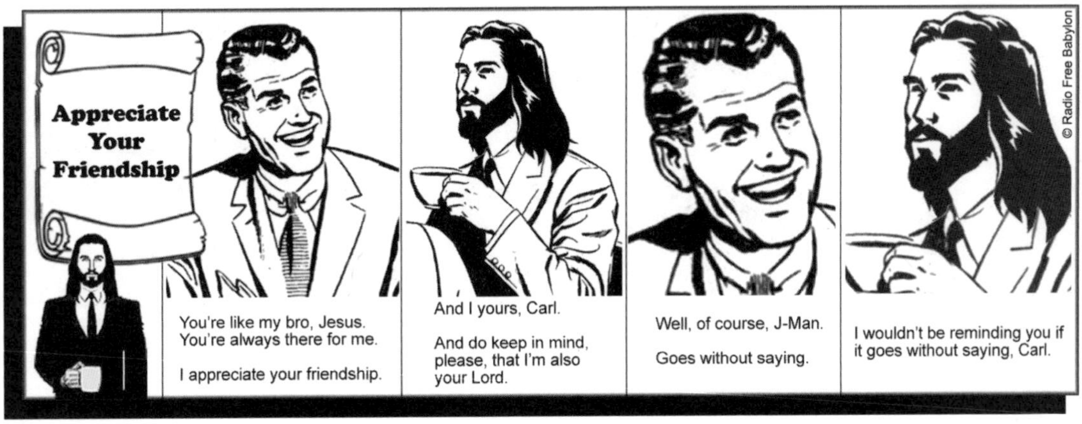
Appreciate Your Friendship
You're like my bro, Jesus. You're always there for me.
I appreciate your friendship.
And I yours, Carl.
And do keep in mind, please, that I'm also your Lord.
Well, of course, J-Man.
Goes without saying.
I wouldn't be reminding you if it goes without saying, Carl.
© Radio Free Babylon

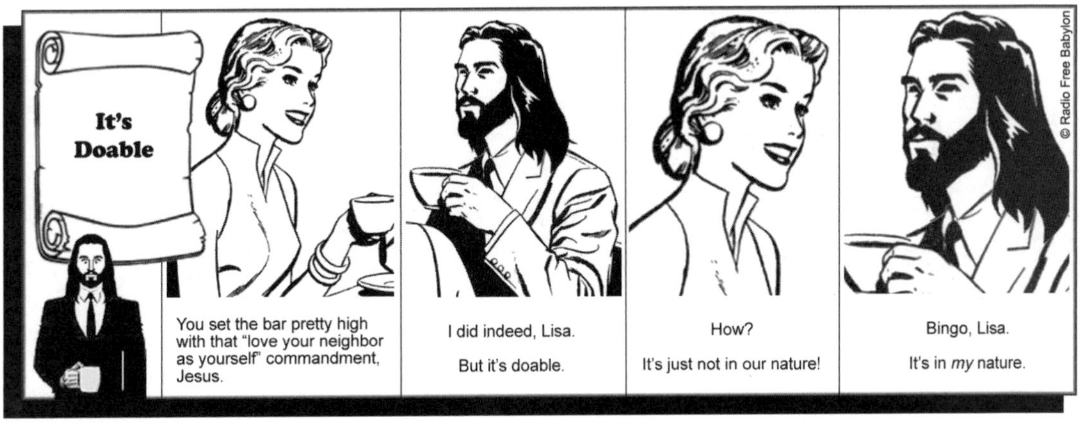
It's Doable
You set the bar pretty high with that "love your neighbor as yourself" commandment, Jesus.
I did indeed, Lisa.
But it's doable.
How?
It's just not in our nature!
Bingo, Lisa.
It's in *my* nature.
© Radio Free Babylon

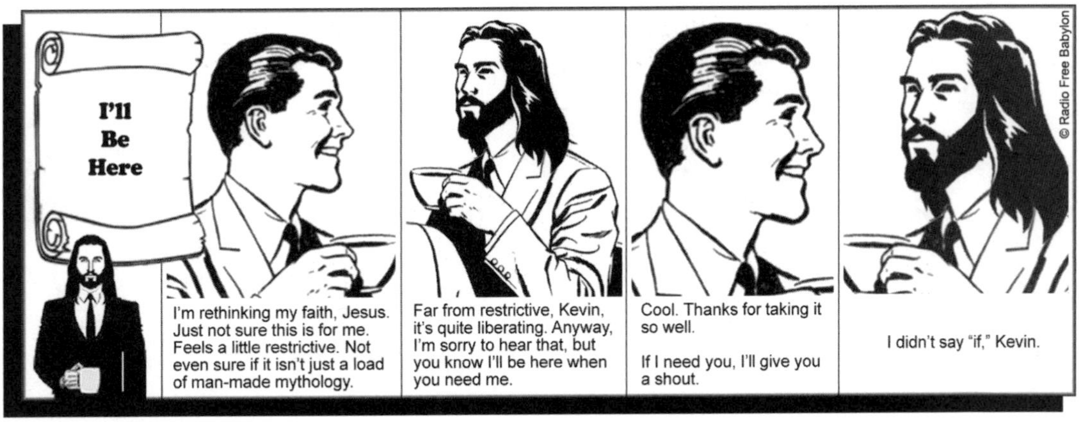
I'll Be Here
I'm rethinking my faith, Jesus. Just not sure this is for me. Feels a little restrictive. Not even sure if it isn't just a load of man-made mythology.
Far from restrictive, Kevin, it's quite liberating. Anyway, I'm sorry to hear that, but you know I'll be here when you need me.
Cool. Thanks for taking it so well.
If I need you, I'll give you a shout.
I didn't say "if," Kevin.
© Radio Free Babylon

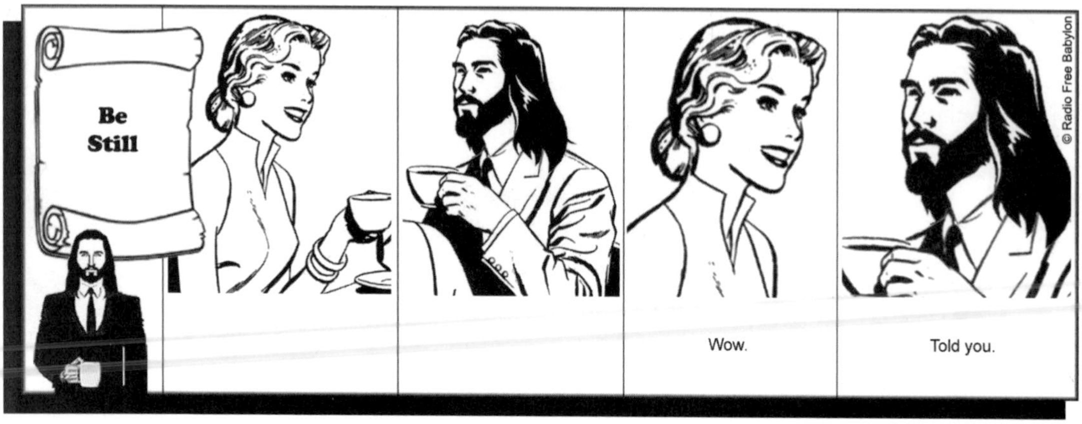
Be Still
Wow.
Told you.
© Radio Free Babylon

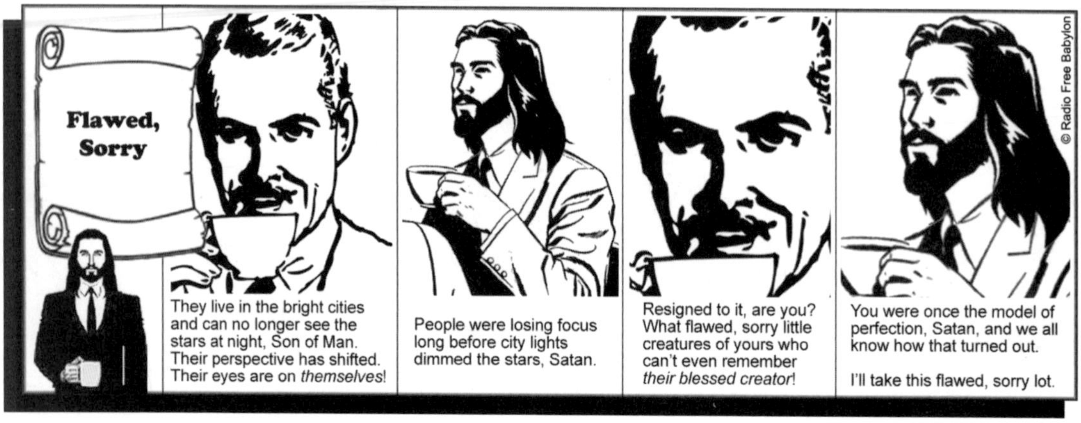
Flawed, Sorry
They live in the bright cities and can no longer see the stars at night, Son of Man. Their perspective has shifted. Their eyes are on *themselves*!
People were losing focus long before city lights dimmed the stars, Satan.
Resigned to it, are you? What flawed, sorry little creatures of yours who can't even remember *their blessed creator*!
You were once the model of perfection, Satan, and we all know how that turned out.
I'll take this flawed, sorry lot.
© Radio Free Babylon

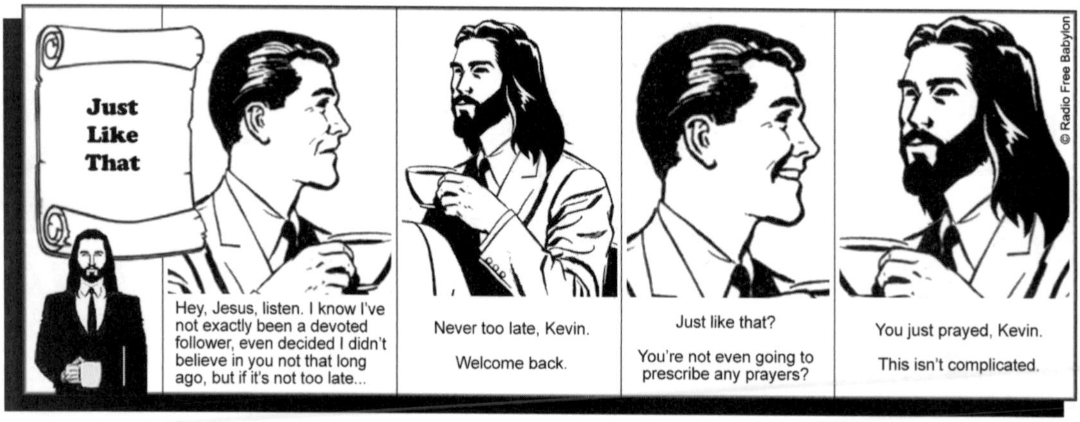
Just Like That
Hey, Jesus, listen. I know I've not exactly been a devoted follower, even decided I didn't believe in you not that long ago, but if it's not too late...
Never too late, Kevin.
Welcome back.
Just like that?
You're not even going to prescribe any prayers?
You just prayed, Kevin.
This isn't complicated.
© Radio Free Babylon

KEVIN

Occupation: Marketing and Advertising
Executive, Church Growth Consultant
Age: 30
Marital Status: Single/Divorced

Kevin came to faith in Jesus at a youth group he was invited to by a girl he liked. She suspected that his commitment was part of a plan to become her boyfriend, and she wasn't wrong. They never dated, and Kevin quickly lost interest in church activities. Even still, Kevin has been haunted, as it were, by Jesus ever since. Though his faith waxes and wanes, Kevin is learning that Jesus pulls no punches, calls him on his antics and can ultimately be trusted.

A professional doubter and cynic, Kevin is always trying to assist churches, and Jesus himself, in becoming more effective communicators.

Kevin married fresh out of college. It didn't last long. He was—and he will tell you this himself—a terrible husband. There was one child from the union, named (naturally) Kevin Jr. He sees his son on weekends and always pays his child support. Kevin now dates, often using Christian dating sites. His relationships still don't last long. His former girlfriends will tell you he's a terrible boyfriend. He's working on it.

2

Who Sees What Is Done in Secret

Spiritual Disciplines

It was a God and Country party, open to all, and those who were not among the faithful knew well that as payment for the free show they'd be hearing plenty of God-talk. They could recite the final invitation in their heads along with the pastor. It always came just before the fireworks:

"With eyes closed and heads bowed, if there's anyone here tonight who has not invited Jesus . . ."

And of course there were "counselors down front" available to those who did invite Jesus. They had been trained earlier in the week at the church's two-hour Counselor Training Class. As soft music played from the stage, they held the new converts' hands and privately counseled them, pressing "Here's What You Do Now" pamphlets into their hands. The rest of the crowd patiently waited for the new converts to hurry back to their places on the grass so the fireworks show could start.

Those who got "plugged in" to the church were going to make it on this long journey, they were told, but those who didn't would fall away. "It's very important that you get plugged in to the church. Doesn't have to be ours, but you'd fit in quite well in the class we have for people of your specific age."

They learned new songs, heard sermons, and joined a class and studied sections of the Bible. They were taught new phrases like "God laid this on my heart," and they learned that to have lunch with another Christian was "fellowshipping." They did good works, and they were quite proud of those good works.

And then one day something ugly dawned on them. They discovered they were religious.

They'd never wanted to be. They'd always hated that word. It smacked of "Scribes, Pharisees, Hypocrites!" They'd become proud. They'd shut up the kingdom of heaven, made it a private club. They walked in arrogance, making a big show of praying over their meals at Applebee's and Denny's after church. They were quick to judge, quick to anger and slow to understand.*

They'd lost the humbleness that had made them answer the invitation that hot July night in the field before the fireworks show all those years ago.

They'd get it back. It would take some doing. They'd start with praying in the car before they walked into Denny's.

*Neil Peart, "Witch Hunt," from the album *Moving Pictures* by Rush (Mercury Records, 1981).

WHO SEES WHAT IS DONE IN SECRET

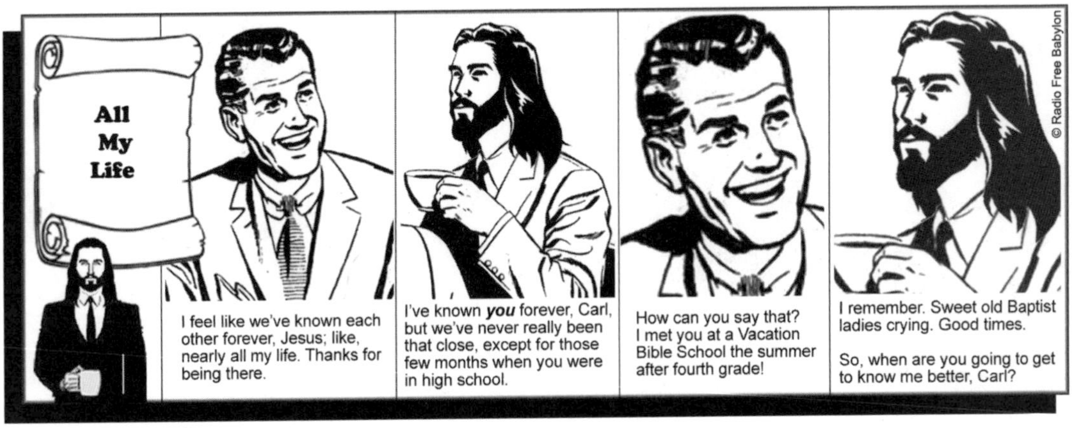
All My Life
I feel like we've known each other forever, Jesus; like, nearly all my life. Thanks for being there.
I've known *you* forever, Carl, but we've never really been that close, except for those few months when you were in high school.
How can you say that? I met you at a Vacation Bible School the summer after fourth grade!
I remember. Sweet old Baptist ladies crying. Good times.
So, when are you going to get to know me better, Carl?
© Radio Free Babylon

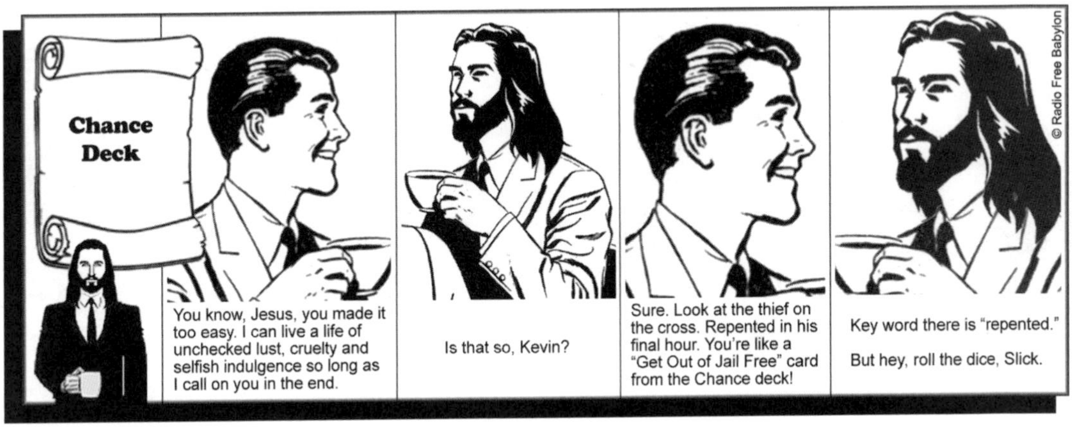
Chance Deck
You know, Jesus, you made it too easy. I can live a life of unchecked lust, cruelty and selfish indulgence so long as I call on you in the end.
Is that so, Kevin?
Sure. Look at the thief on the cross. Repented in his final hour. You're like a "Get Out of Jail Free" card from the Chance deck!
Key word there is "repented."
But hey, roll the dice, Slick.
© Radio Free Babylon

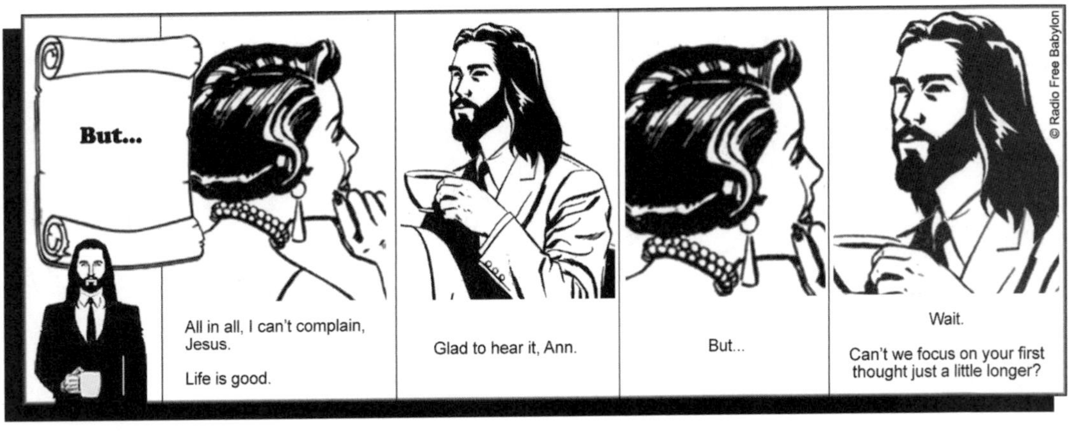
But...
All in all, I can't complain, Jesus.
Life is good.
Glad to hear it, Ann.
But...
Wait.
Can't we focus on your first thought just a little longer?
© Radio Free Babylon

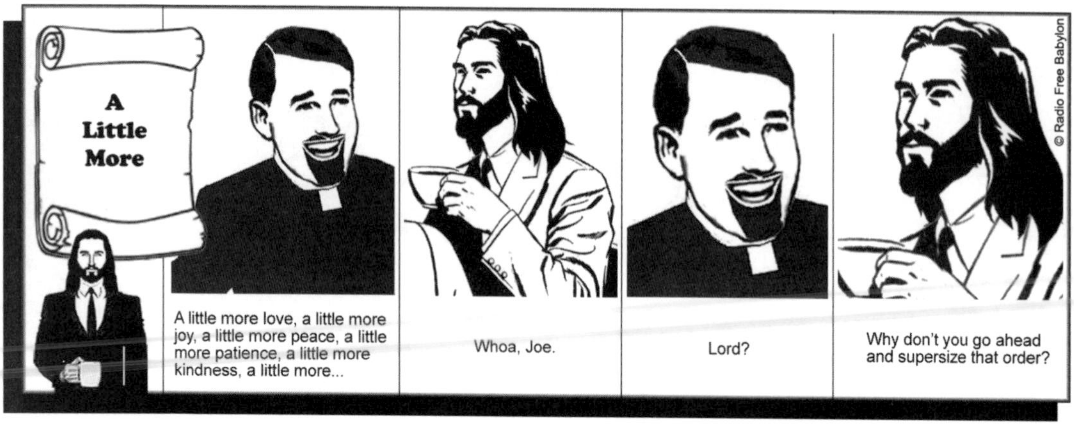
A Little More
A little more love, a little more joy, a little more peace, a little more patience, a little more kindness, a little more...
Whoa, Joe.
Lord?
Why don't you go ahead and supersize that order?
© Radio Free Babylon

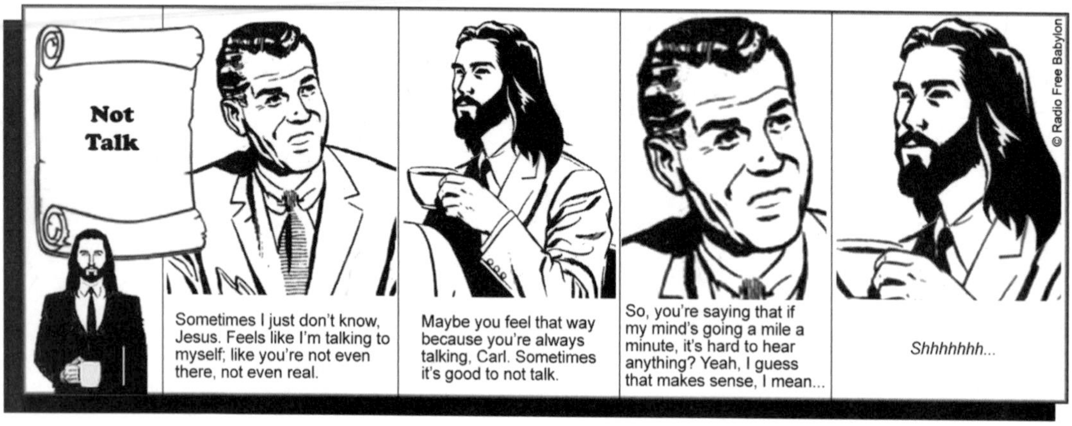
Not Talk
Sometimes I just don't know, Jesus. Feels like I'm talking to myself; like you're not even there, not even real.
Maybe you feel that way because you're always talking, Carl. Sometimes it's good to not talk.
So, you're saying that if my mind's going a mile a minute, it's hard to hear anything? Yeah, I guess that makes sense, I mean...
Shhhhhhh...
© Radio Free Babylon

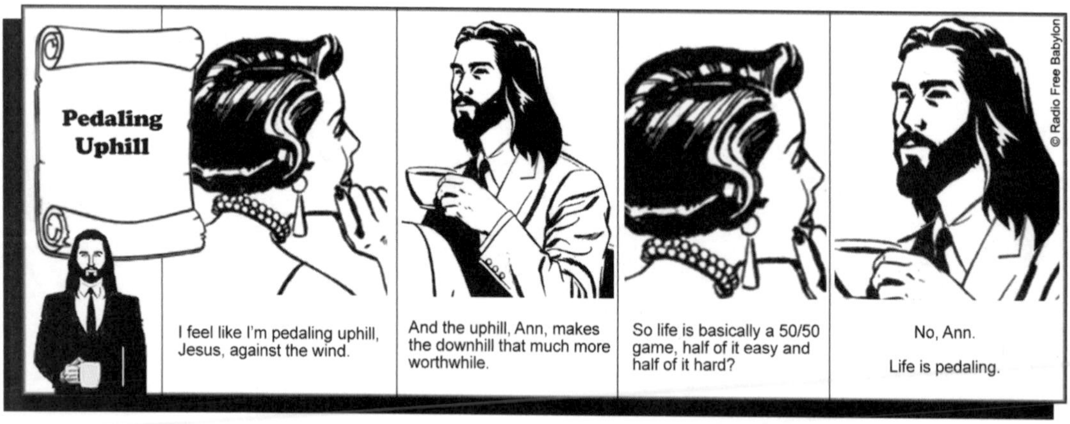
Pedaling Uphill
I feel like I'm pedaling uphill, Jesus, against the wind.
And the uphill, Ann, makes the downhill that much more worthwhile.
So life is basically a 50/50 game, half of it easy and half of it hard?
No, Ann.
Life is pedaling.
© Radio Free Babylon

Hear from You

I really need to hear from you on that thing I've been asking you about, Jesus.

And you will, Lisa.

Well, that's good to know.

When will I get my answer?

When you quit imagining that the answer is "yes."

Spiritual

I really wouldn't consider myself "religious." I'm just *spiritual*, you know?

Everyone is "spiritual," Ann.

Oh, you know what I mean, Jesus. I just don't want to be pigeonholed into one of the ugly stereotypes people have in their minds.

Sure, like the stereotype of the person who says they are "spiritual" as being kind of wishy-washy and open to anything?

Where's the Love?

Christians aren't perfect, just forgiven.

Right, J-Man?

Right again, Carl. And let me guess; God is your copilot? And your boss is a Jewish carpenter?

Man, whenever I try to share something with you, why you always gotta be so sarcastic and mocking? Where's the love, Jesus?

Still love you, Carl. But if your grown son was talking like a two-year-old well into his forties, don't you think you'd want to smack him around just a little?

Tired Old Saying

Not a good day, Jesus.

I'm just mad this morning.

You were mad last night, too.

Don't let the sun go down on your anger, Kevin.

Oh, please. Life's a little more complex than that.

That tired old saying belongs in a fortune cookie.

Sure does. So tape it to your bathroom mirror and you'll be reminded of it as you're angrily brushing your teeth before bed, Kevin.

Carpe Diem

Got a mower full of gas, the sun is shining, the birds are singing! The world is RIGHT! Let's go mow some lawns, Jesus! C'mon! *Carpe Diem!*

You need to quit *carpe*-ing the Five Hour Energy shots, Carl. But your new attitude is refreshing.

Yeah, J-Man, I've got an *attitude of gratitude!* Today is nothing but possibilities! Ain't nothing gonna bring me down!

Don't bet on that, brother. A couple of hours in your truck listening to AM talk radio should have you mad at the world all over again.

A Personal Word

I need to hear from you, Jesus. A personal word that directly speaks to my life, so that I know I'm hearing from you and not my imagination.

Give yourself up, Ann.

Too personal?

– 38 –

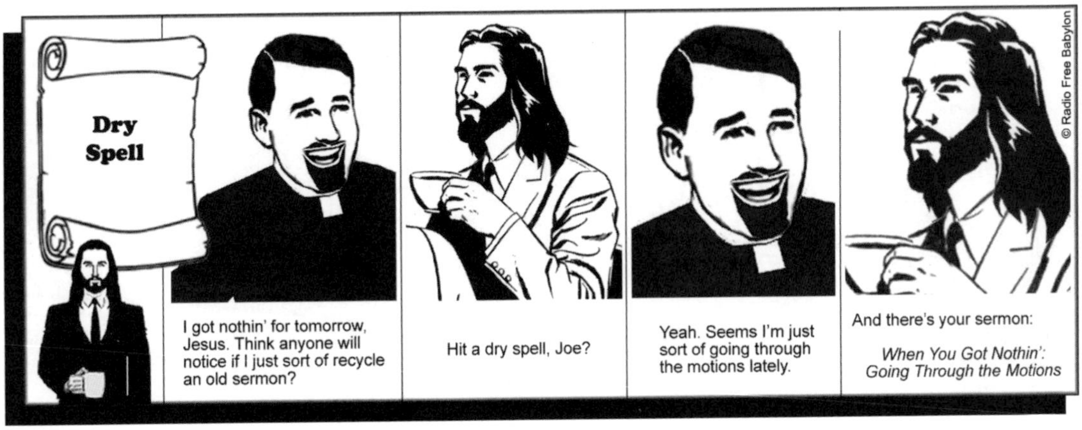
Dry Spell
© Radio Free Babylon
I got nothin' for tomorrow, Jesus. Think anyone will notice if I just sort of recycle an old sermon?
Hit a dry spell, Joe?
Yeah. Seems I'm just sort of going through the motions lately.
And there's your sermon:
When You Got Nothin': Going Through the Motions

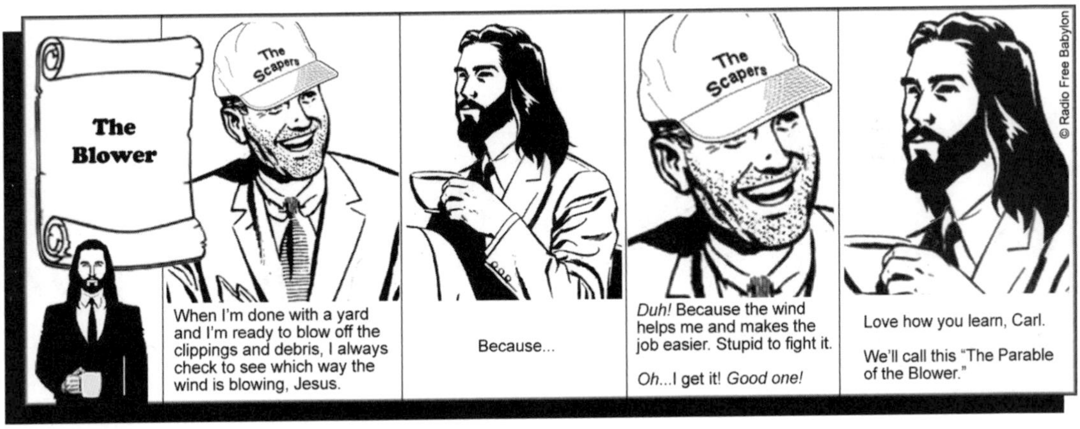
The Blower
© Radio Free Babylon
The Scapers
When I'm done with a yard and I'm ready to blow off the clippings and debris, I always check to see which way the wind is blowing, Jesus.
Because...
The Scapers
Duh! Because the wind helps me and makes the job easier. Stupid to fight it.
Oh...I get it! *Good one!*
Love how you learn, Carl.
We'll call this "The Parable of the Blower."

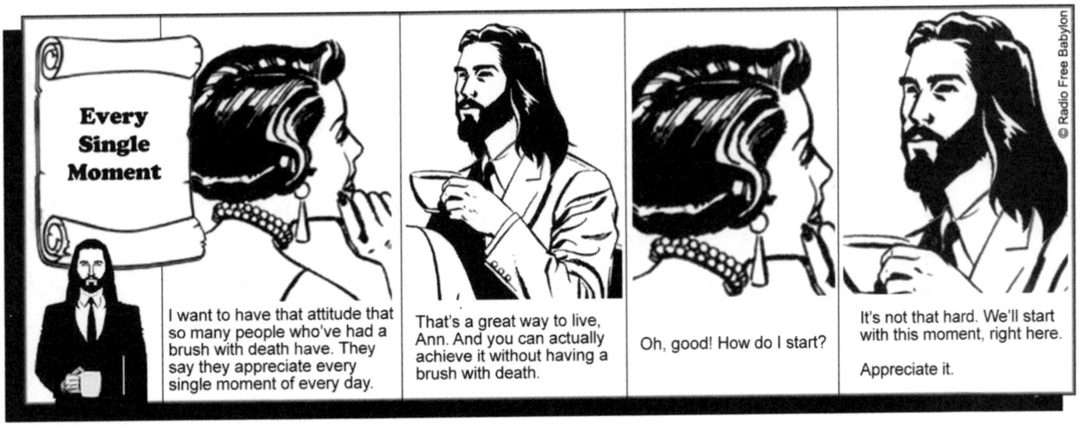
Every Single Moment
© Radio Free Babylon
I want to have that attitude that so many people who've had a brush with death have. They say they appreciate every single moment of every day.
That's a great way to live, Ann. And you can actually achieve it without having a brush with death.
Oh, good! How do I start?
It's not that hard. We'll start with this moment, right here.
Appreciate it.

Someone's Always Watching

They say integrity is what you do when no one is watching.

Even if I didn't exist, Kevin, someone's always watching.

Yeah, you wanna be able to look that person in the mirror straight in the eye, right?

Exactly.

But perhaps with a little less posing and flexing in your case, Kevin.

Distracted

Does it annoy you that I sometimes get distracted when we're talking, Jesus?

You have a busy life, Ann. It's easy to lose focus.

It's not annoying, no.

Report done by noon... Milk, eggs, pasta, dog food...oil change overdue! Oh, crap! Forgot to call my sister.

I'll still be here when you're done, Ann.

Take your time.

Amen Isn't Goodbye

Remember that night in the garden before they came to arrest you and your buddies kept falling asleep?

I only asked them to stay awake for an hour, Carl.

But, you know, they'd had a big dinner, it was late.

Well, I'm thinking if your closest friends couldn't pray for an hour, then a guy like me is doing pretty good to give you five minutes, right?

Just because you've said, "Amen," Carl, doesn't mean we have to say, "Goodbye."

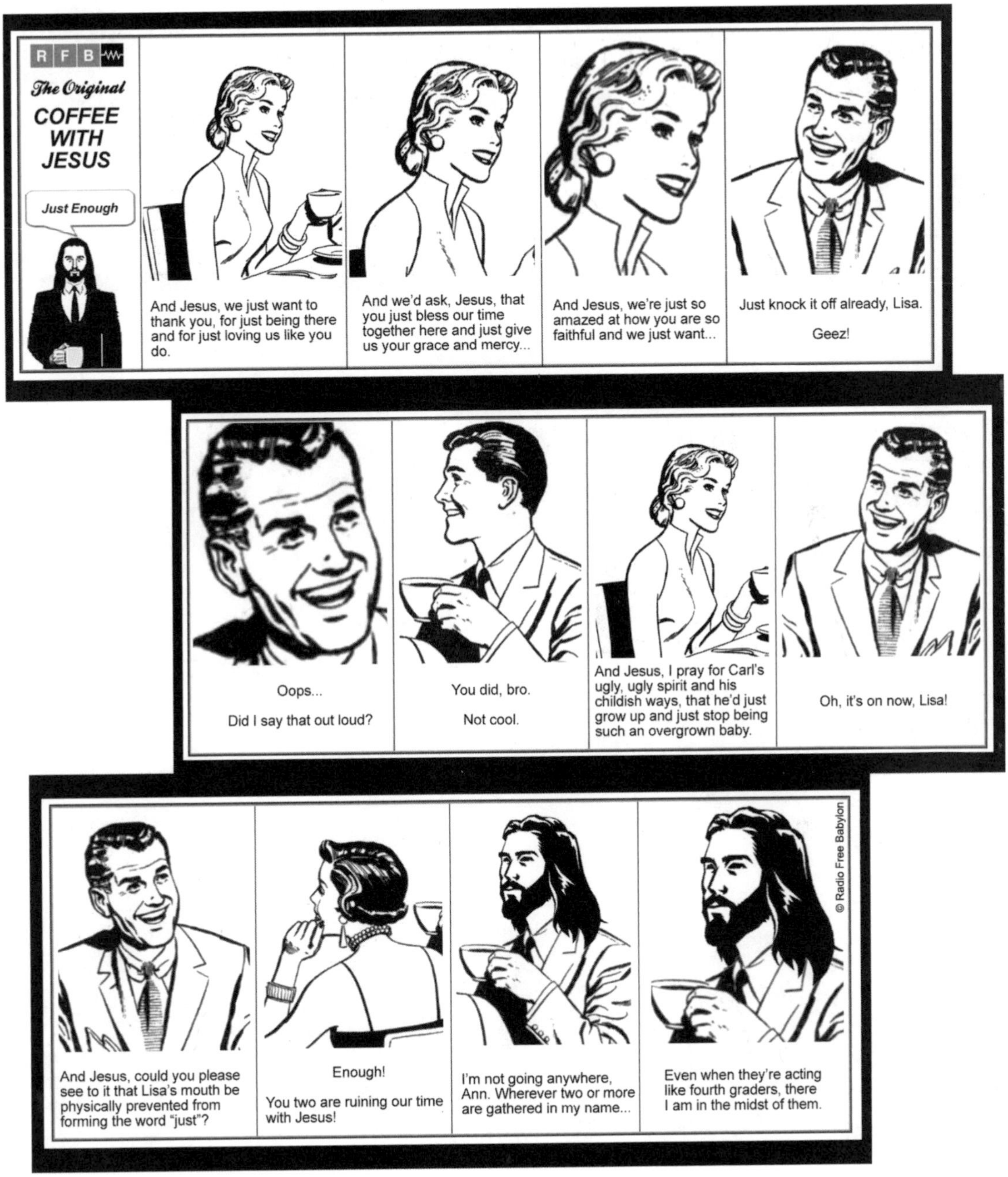
R F B
The Original
COFFEE WITH JESUS
Just Enough
And Jesus, we just want to thank you, for just being there and for just loving us like you do.
And we'd ask, Jesus, that you just bless our time together here and just give us your grace and mercy...
And Jesus, we're just so amazed at how you are so faithful and we just want...
Just knock it off already, Lisa.
Geez!
Oops...
Did I say that out loud?
You did, bro.
Not cool.
And Jesus, I pray for Carl's ugly, ugly spirit and his childish ways, that he'd just grow up and just stop being such an overgrown baby.
Oh, it's on now, Lisa!
And Jesus, could you please see to it that Lisa's mouth be physically prevented from forming the word "just"?
Enough!
You two are ruining our time with Jesus!
I'm not going anywhere, Ann. Wherever two or more are gathered in my name...
Even when they're acting like fourth graders, there I am in the midst of them.
© Radio Free Babylon

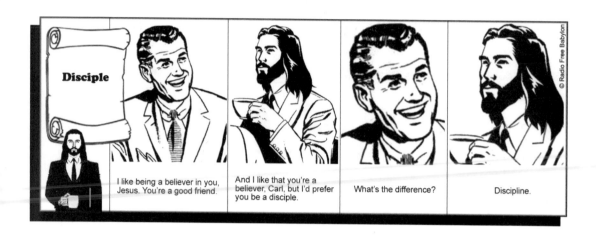

Disciple

I like being a believer in you, Jesus. You're a good friend.

And I like that you're a believer, Carl, but I'd prefer you be a disciple.

What's the difference?

Discipline.

Faith and Works

The Bible says that "faith without works is dead," Jesus. But in other places it says that faith is all I need.

You seem to think there's a contradiction, Kevin.

Faith will *produce* works.

So if I have faith I will just naturally do good works?

Not naturally.

Supernaturally.

If Then

Remember that time I promised to always live for you if you got me out of that horrible jam?

Actually, Ann, you've thrown that one at me quite a few times. I call it the "If Then" prayer. Hear them all the time.

Well, the thing is, I haven't been too faithful in holding up my end of the bargain.

Very few people are, Ann. So I have an "If Then" for you. If you quit trying to bargain with me, then you can stop thinking of me as a pawn broker.

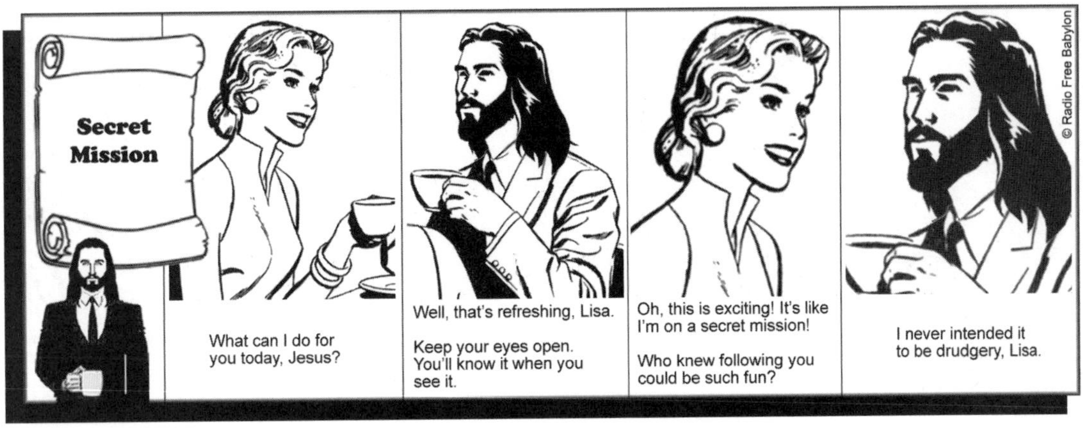
Secret Mission
What can I do for you today, Jesus?
Well, that's refreshing, Lisa.
Keep your eyes open. You'll know it when you see it.
Oh, this is exciting! It's like I'm on a secret mission!
Who knew following you could be such fun?
I never intended it to be drudgery, Lisa.
© Radio Free Babylon

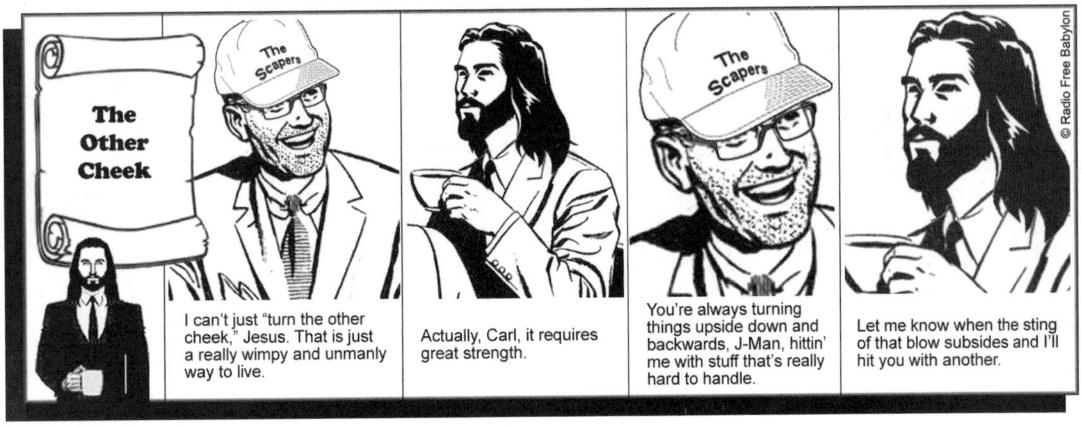
The Other Cheek
The Scapers
I can't just "turn the other cheek," Jesus. That is just a really wimpy and unmanly way to live.
Actually, Carl, it requires great strength.
The Scapers
You're always turning things upside down and backwards, J-Man, hittin' me with stuff that's really hard to handle.
Let me know when the sting of that blow subsides and I'll hit you with another.
© Radio Free Babylon

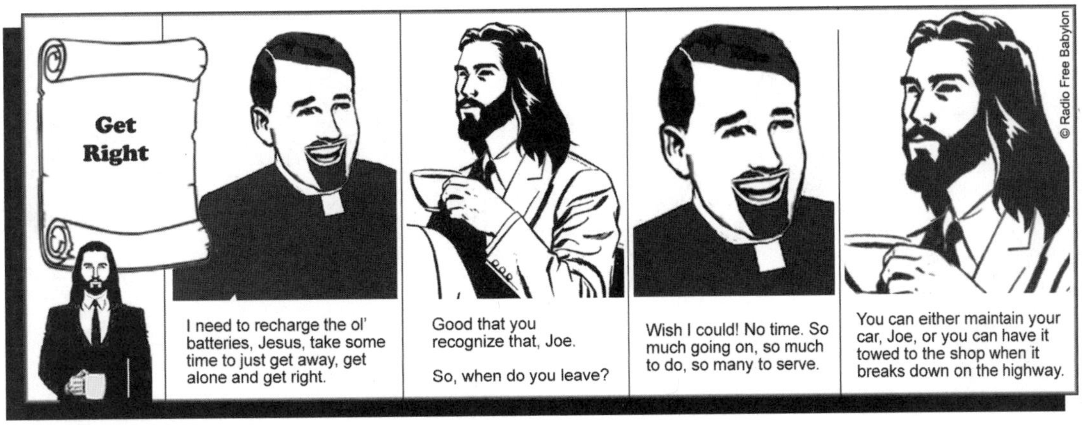
Get Right
I need to recharge the ol' batteries, Jesus, take some time to just get away, get alone and get right.
Good that you recognize that, Joe.
So, when do you leave?
Wish I could! No time. So much going on, so much to do, so many to serve.
You can either maintain your car, Joe, or you can have it towed to the shop when it breaks down on the highway.
© Radio Free Babylon

Donate Some Stuff

The scouts are having their annual food drive.

Think I'll donate some stuff. Feels good to help others.

And by "some stuff," you mean some rusty cans of turnip greens and other things you were never going to eat?

Hey, beggars can't be choosers, right?

And isn't it the thought that counts?

Your thoughtfulness has been noted, Kevin.

Crazy at Work

Things are just crazy at work these days, Jesus. I can barely keep up.

One time, Joseph got an order for fourteen doors for this rich guy's house and the guy wanted them finished within an impossible deadline.

Oh, I think I read about this in *The Lost Books of the Bible*. So you just sort of used your power and saved the day, right?

No. We busted our butts until the job was done. It's called "work," Carl. Be thankful you have a job.

Change My Situation

Why isn't my situation changing, Jesus?

What are you doing to change your situation, Ann?

Waiting on you to change my situation, Jesus!

That's another situation that needs to change, Ann.

Needy

Why do you require worship, Jesus? It seems sort of, I don't know another way to put this, sort of *needy* on your part.

You worship rock stars, sports heroes, nature, the human body, Kevin.

And you get angry if we put those things ahead of you, am I right?

More sad than angry, Kevin, because I'm not the one who needs it. You are.

Think About It

I sometimes wonder if when I think I'm hearing your voice, I'm really just hearing what I want to hear, Jesus.

What was the last thing you thought you heard me say?

It was, *"Lisa, go to the spa. You've had a hard week and you deserve it."* But now that I think about it, that wasn't you, was it?

Helps to think about it, doesn't it, Lisa?

Mature a Little

God bless Mommy and Daddy and Grandma and Grandpa and Aunt Alice and Uncle Jim and the other Grandma and Grandpa and my sister Lucy...

Carl, seriously, it's time for your prayers to mature a little.

What do you mean, J-Man?

I've been praying this way my whole life.

Exactly.

Those Long Spaces

Wake up, go to work, come home, make dinner, watch TV, go to sleep. *Soooo* tired of this routine, Jesus.

Life gets dull, Ann, if you're just looking at it as a series of boring days that never end.

It sure seems that way a lot of the time, Jesus.

Please help me to *not* look at it that way.

Life is lived mainly in those long spaces between the peaks and valleys, Ann. Best not to wait for joy or sorrow to make you feel alive.

Thanks

Sometimes when I get to the "thanks" part of my prayers, I just start reciting stuff I know I'm *supposed* to be thankful for, Jesus.

Perhaps you're taking those things for granted, Lisa.

How do I not do that?

Imagine losing them.

Again. Again.

And that's what I did, Jesus. I'm sorry and I'm gonna try not to do it again...again.

Forgive me?

You got it, Carl.

Serious?

As long as you are.

CARL

Occupation: Owner, The Scapers, a lawn
maintenance/landscaping company
Age: 44
Marital Status: Married

Even the people who don't like Carl will say things like, "You gotta love ol' Carl." He's one of the boys. Carl first ran into Jesus at Vacation Bible School the summer after fourth grade. Today, both emotionally and spiritually, Carl is still very much a fourth grader.

Carl started his landscaping company after being fired from numerous jobs. He worked in timeshares, was briefly a greeter at Walmart, did some seasonal work in The Home Depot's Christmas tree tent, and managed his friend Jake's restaurant, Jake's Wing House, where he developed a full-blown midlife crisis, the remnants of which still ocassionally appear in the form of cool glasses, an earring and facial hair. In too many cases, Carl's wandering eye was not appreciated by his coworkers. Though he would never be unfaithful to his wife, his eye was nonetheless offensive. Jesus agreed that solitary work might be Carl's best option.

He's making decent money and is a firm believer in "bringing home the bacon" for his wife, Lisa, a stay-at-home mom. With two children in college and one in elementary school ("the accident," they call him), Carl and Lisa have been together since college, when Lisa became pregnant (also known as "the accident").

Carl's political and religious views are fused, and he'd have no problem telling you that if you don't vote the way he does, you're obviously not a Christian and you should maybe just leave the country.

3

Do to Others

Relationships

Every conflict, it has been said, comes about as a result of one party feeling that they have not received from another party what was due them. Respect, property, money, sex, a promised report, the lawn mowed, the dishwasher emptied, the land taken in wartime. Whatever the perceived injustice, whether huge or small, it's making someone mad—and it's probably huge in their eyes. In a family, in a company, in a country: where there's conflict, somebody at least *thinks* they've been done wrong.

And so Jesus said, "Here's the Old Testament summed up for you: Put yourself in the other person's shoes."

Easier said. Good one, Jesus.

Spouses, children, coworkers, neighbors, that punk on the interstate driving like an idiot . . . There are opportunities for conflict everywhere. "I wouldn't drive like that!" "I wouldn't let my yard look like that!" "I wouldn't turn in work that looked like that!" "I wouldn't sass my mother like that!" "I wouldn't be grumpy for no good reason like that!"

Yeah, you would. And you have.

That other person's shoes are too small or too big. That other person's shoes are not my color, and besides, they're *waaaay* out of style. Look at 'em! Who'd even *buy* a pair of shoes like that?

Forgive me for resorting to another lyric I wrote. This one's called "Broken Bread."

> Everyone I meet makes me smile
> they make me smile
> most of them, anyway
> it only takes a little while
> just a while
> to see past the cold and gray

COFFEE WITH JESUS

And what I don't like in you
is what I hate about me
the things that you are
the way you can be
cold or just cool with a selfish streak
man, I see that in me

I want a prescription for x-ray vision
and you need to learn to bend steel
maybe we could leap some tall buildings
and in a single bound
we would feel the real deal

I think I'll order the broken bread
we can split the two-for-one meal
I'll try to keep my elbows off the table
and in a single bite
I'll bet we'd taste the real deal

And there might be a few
there might be two or three
who aren't quite mirrors
and you can't quite see
shield your eyes or they'll make you weak
straining so hard, yeah I see it in me

I'm not offering a deal
and you don't need to make a trade
like I'll dance in your sun
if you'll walk in my shade
hot or just warm with a soft breeze
yeah, I see you in me

I want a prescription for x-ray vision
and you need to learn to bend steel
maybe we could crash some stone gates
and in a single bound
we would feel the real deal

Go on and order the broken bread
we'll split the two-for-one meal
we'll find a hot sauce we both can stand
and in a single bite
I'll bet we taste the real deal

World Peace

So many people pray for world peace, Jesus. Why aren't you making that happen?

I'm working on it, Ann. It will come in time. A lot of things have to happen first. There's a process to this.

Thy kingdom come, right? Thy will be done, right? We've been praying that for two thousand years!

How about you learn to get along with your coworkers and your ex-husband first? World peace is a few years off, sister.

'Fraid So, Bro

Give me this day my daily bread, and forgive me my trespasses.

As you forgive those who trespass against you, Kevin.

You can't *possibly* mean my former business partner who cost me thousands of dollars in back taxes due to his stupid negligence!

'Fraid so, bro.

Bitter pill at first, I know, but it'll cure what ails you.

A Few Others

Do people pray for me, Jesus?

Sure. There's your mom, your wife, of course (though she wearies as her prayers don't seem to effect change), a few others, Carl.

Well, that's encouraging.

Can you tell me the most recent prayer made on my behalf?

Well, technically not "prayers," really, but a few drivers of the cars you cut off on the highway this morning specifically asked that I damn you.

Attitude

When our boys lose their soccer games, we always tell them, "It's not whether you win or lose. It's how you play the game."

Kids love to win, but yeah, giving it your best effort is huge with me. I love a player with a good attitude who goes all out.

I just wish our team could win more often. The poor little guys get so down after a loss. Can you, *maybe, you know*...help out?

Raising Lazarus would be easy by comparison, Lisa. They're just no good. But great job on the attitude development.

Bless His Heart

My brother-in-law has never really been able to find his place within our family. The man is just *soooo* awkward, bless his heart.

Gladly, Ann.

Consider his heart blessed.

No, Jesus, that's just what the women in my family say when we mean, "That man is a piece of work. *What* did she ever see in him?"

Too late. His heart is blessed, and now he will outlive every last one of you.

Church Marquee

I don't know what's happened to me, Jesus, but I'm getting more and more bitter every day. Just *angry* all the time!

Well, I told him, *"An attitude of gratitude will wipe the snarl off of Carl,"* Jesus.

Cute, isn't she, Jesus?

A walking church marquee.

Carl, c'mon.

Be grateful, not hateful.

Energy Vampires

I've decided I'm getting rid of the negative people in my life, Jesus. I want to be positive and surround myself with positive people.

So you will love the lovely, Kevin?

You will bring light to the light and joy to the joyful?

But they rub off on you and bring you down, Jesus. It's best to just avoid them.

They're energy vampires.

And you risk becoming one of the walking dead, Kevin.

Regular Family Stuff

I can't even talk to my brother anymore, Jesus. We end up in heated political arguments. It's because he gets all his news from that one network.

And you get all your news from that other one, Lisa.

Here's an idea: don't talk politics with your brother.

So what, we just talk about regular family stuff and pretend the elephant isn't in the room?

Yep. And the donkey too.

No Secrets, No Lies

Lisa and I have always tried to maintain a very honest and open relationship, Jesus. *"No secrets, no lies"* is our motto.

That's healthy, Carl.

It takes work to maintain a good marriage.

So...how do I tell her she's gained a little weight, J-Man?

There's a time to speak and a time to be silent, Carl.

Guess which time this is?

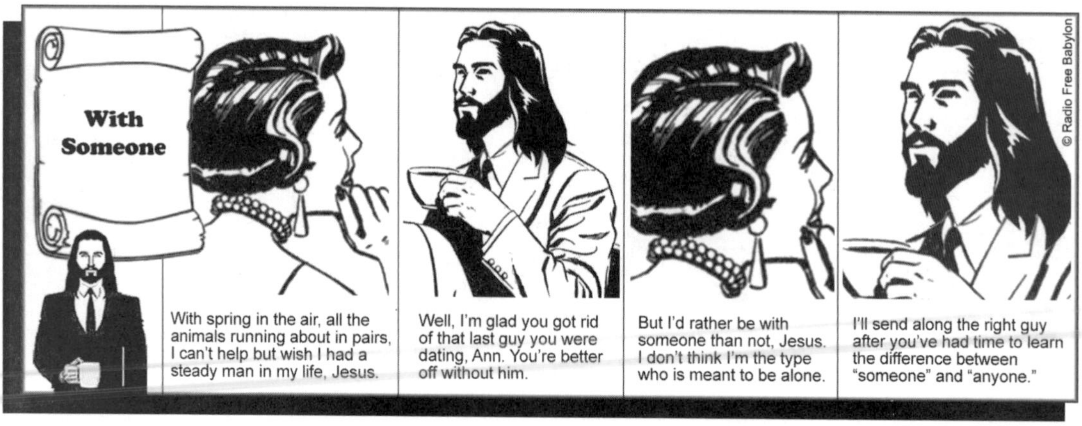
With Someone
With spring in the air, all the animals running about in pairs, I can't help but wish I had a steady man in my life, Jesus.
Well, I'm glad you got rid of that last guy you were dating, Ann. You're better off without him.
But I'd rather be with someone than not, Jesus. I don't think I'm the type who is meant to be alone.
I'll send along the right guy after you've had time to learn the difference between "someone" and "anyone."
© Radio Free Babylon

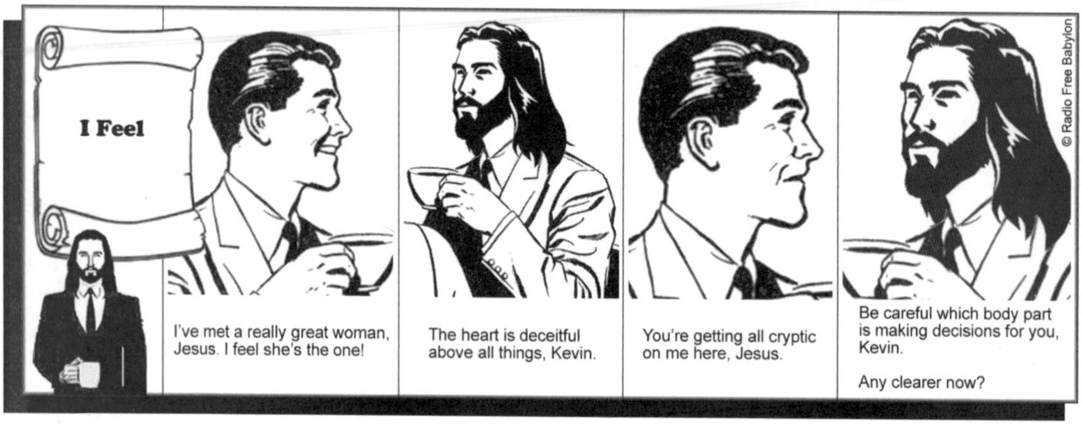
I Feel
I've met a really great woman, Jesus. I feel she's the one!
The heart is deceitful above all things, Kevin.
You're getting all cryptic on me here, Jesus.
Be careful which body part is making decisions for you, Kevin.
Any clearer now?
© Radio Free Babylon

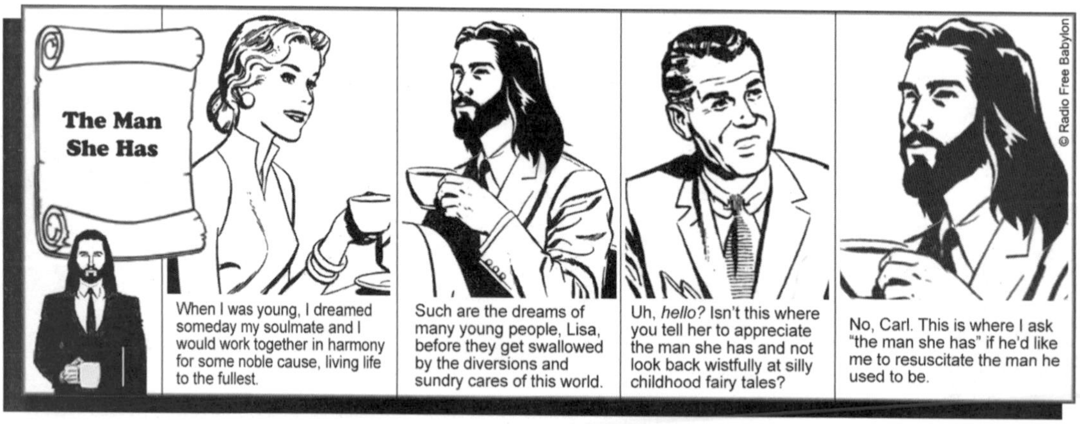
The Man She Has
When I was young, I dreamed someday my soulmate and I would work together in harmony for some noble cause, living life to the fullest.
Such are the dreams of many young people, Lisa, before they get swallowed by the diversions and sundry cares of this world.
Uh, *hello?* Isn't this where you tell her to appreciate the man she has and not look back wistfully at silly childhood fairy tales?
No, Carl. This is where I ask "the man she has" if he'd like me to resuscitate the man he used to be.
© Radio Free Babylon

A Good Front

You ever compare the image on the ads for a Big Mac with what you *actually get* when you order a Big Mac? It's a deflated pile of soggy mess.

I'm more of a Filet-o-Fish guy, but I know what you mean, Kevin. People are always putting up a good front in order to fool others.

OK, I know what you're going to say, and I want you to know that I put up a more current profile picture on the Christian dating site.

And "Skydiving, snowboarding and sailing" *sound like* manly interests, but they're just dreams. Maybe you can fix those? You feel me, Big Mac?

Things That Don't Matter

Remember that woman at work, the one I can't stand? We went to lunch yesterday. Funny, we actually have a lot in common.

Funny, yes. And I liked how you didn't react visibly to her less-than-refined table manners. I know how that bugs you.

OMG! That took *everything* in me! It was making me *crazy.*

Keep this up, Ann, and you're going to be able to see past all kinds of things that don't matter.

Serious Trust Issues

Lisa's been checking my emails again and scouring the phone records, Jesus. We have serious trust issues.

You have a history of being untrustworthy, Carl. So, Lisa, what prompted this new round of snooping on Carl?

I caught him reading my copy of *Fifty Shades of Gray.* What man would do that unless his mistress asked him to?

That's some crazy logic, Lisa, but how about we put that book in the trash where it belongs and regroup in a week.

© Radio Free Babylon

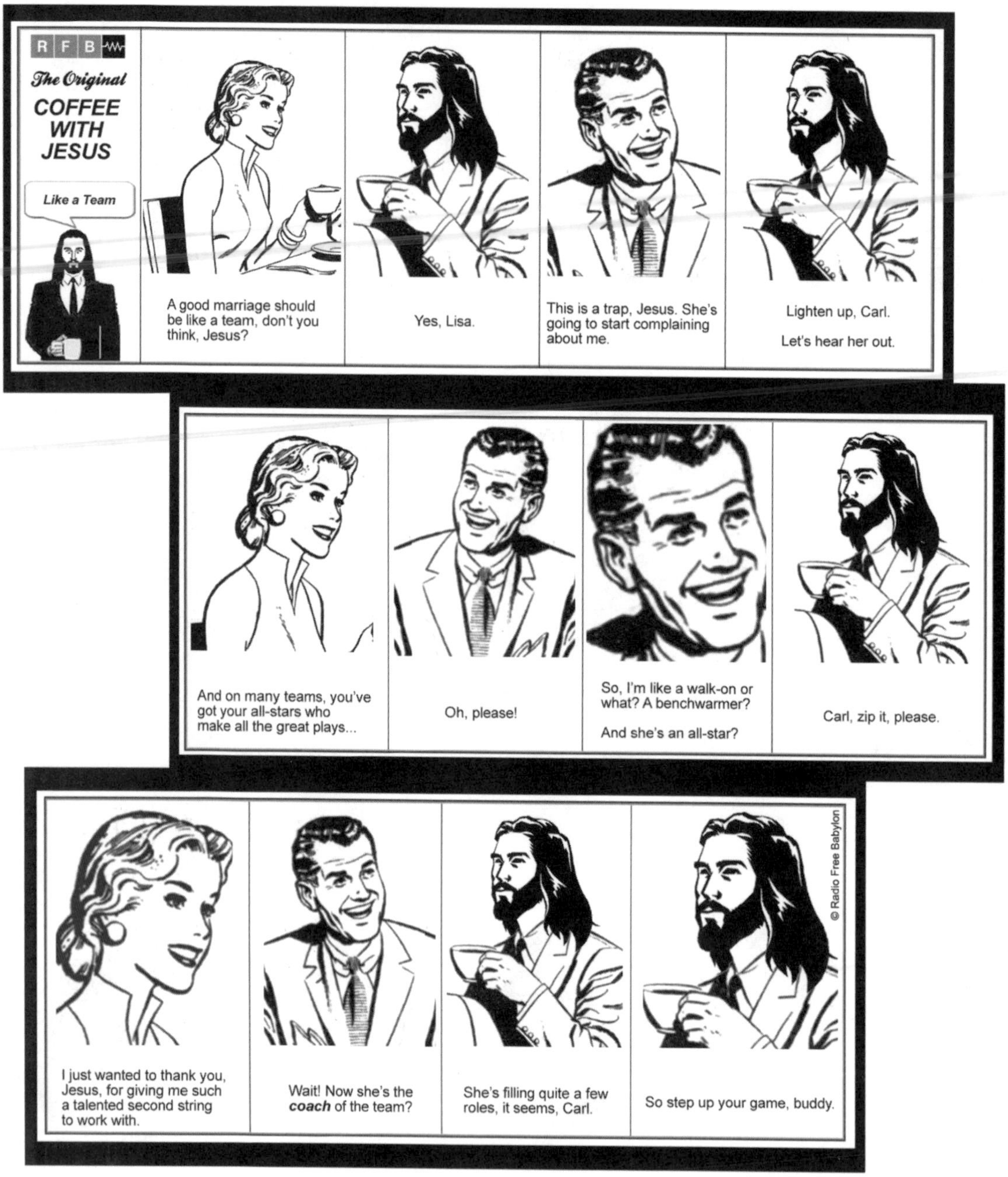
RFB
The Original
COFFEE WITH JESUS
Like a Team
A good marriage should be like a team, don't you think, Jesus?
Yes, Lisa.
This is a trap, Jesus. She's going to start complaining about me.
Lighten up, Carl.
Let's hear her out.
And on many teams, you've got your all-stars who make all the great plays...
Oh, please!
So, I'm like a walk-on or what? A benchwarmer?
And she's an all-star?
Carl, zip it, please.
I just wanted to thank you, Jesus, for giving me such a talented second string to work with.
Wait! Now she's the ***coach*** of the team?
She's filling quite a few roles, it seems, Carl.
So step up your game, buddy.
© Radio Free Babylon

Gimme a Shout

That old hymn is true, Jesus. *"Morning by morning new mercies I see."* But then I lose sight of them by the afternoon.

Not uncommon, Ann.

When you feel yourself getting mired in the muck of the day, gimme a shout.

And you'll keep me from giving in to my angry, cynical side?

I'll at least try to keep you from showing that side to your coworkers.

© Radio Free Babylon

Jealousy

Part One

Carl is such a jealous man, Jesus. It puts an incredible strain on our marriage. I wish he'd be more trusting.

When Carl asked you to join the Y with him and give up your personal trainer, how did you respond, Lisa?

I said I get a much better workout when someone like Antonio is pushing me—someone who has spent a lot of time learning my body.

Yeah, see, statements like that aren't very reassuring to a jealous man.

© Radio Free Babylon

What's My Problem?

The words of my ex-wife still ring in my head, "You're the worst husband in the world."

Was I that bad, Jesus?

Worst in the world? Of course not, Kevin.

She was exaggerating… slightly.

And my last three girl-friends all left me!

What's my *problem*?

I can answer that with an old children's rhyme: *Kevin and Kevin, sittin' in a tree, K-I-S-S-I-N-G.*

© Radio Free Babylon

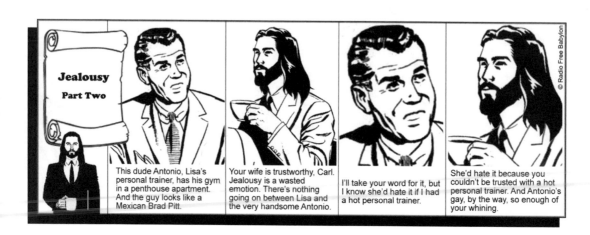

Jealousy Part Two

This dude Antonio, Lisa's personal trainer, has his gym in a penthouse apartment. And the guy looks like a Mexican Brad Pitt.

Your wife is trustworthy, Carl. Jealousy is a wasted emotion. There's nothing going on between Lisa and the very handsome Antonio.

I'll take your word for it, but I know she'd hate it if I had a hot personal trainer.

She'd hate it because you couldn't be trusted with a hot personal trainer. And Antonio's gay, by the way, so enough of your whining.

Let This Cup Pass

You know what I want, Jesus, and I've asked you for it many times, but it doesn't happen.

You're talking to someone who knows this area well, Ann. I asked, "If it's possible, let this cup pass from me."

This is a little different, don't you think, Jesus?

It's not like I'm about to die for the sins of the world.

Still, Ann, my dying an excruciating, lonely death and you not finding a super-fit, rich, dancing, cooking Christian man have a higher purpose.

Gave Yourself Up

Jesus, do you think you could remind Lisa what the Bible says about wives submitting to their husbands?

He always forgets the next part about husbands loving their wives as you loved the church, Jesus, and gave yourself up for it.

Yeah? Who emptied the dishwasher last night...

...without being asked?

And Jesus wept.

Curb Appeal

A house on the block with a trashy yard, peeling paint and dirty cars is ruining the curb appeal of our home, Jesus. It's upsetting.

Caroline has been in the hospital for two months and James has been spending his days at her side, Lisa.

Oh. Caroline and James.

Now that I know their names, I'll remember them in my prayers.

You do that, neighbor. And organize a crew to tidy up the place. And bring James some food. Give him a break from hospital cafeteria junk.

Wild Ride

That young couple who asked me to officiate at their wedding, Jesus, I just don't think they're ready.

They're not, Joe.

But who ever is?

Is it OK if I tell them that you said they're not ready?

It won't stop them, Joe. Let them know they're in for a wild ride, then preside and step aside.

Like His Dad

Our youngest son has been getting into trouble at school, Jesus. Seems he's a bit of a class clown.

He *is* funny, that kid.

But yes, he needs to show respect and learn to keep his mouth shut during class.

Or his teacher needs to lighten up and recognize the kid's a comedic genius, just like his dad!

Said the man whose humor hasn't changed much since he was about the same age.

Make Someone Smile

I'm going to make someone smile today, Jesus. That's my new project. Somewhere out there is a frown I'm going to turn upside down!

That's sweet, Lisa.

Charity starts at home, Little Miss Cheer Spreader.

And has it occurred to you where your wife got the idea for this new project of hers, Carl?

Let Us Down

One of my employees called in sick, Jesus, and then later that day I saw him walking into the theater with his family.

Are you going to ask him about it, Ann?

Well, it's his sick day to waste, but I was sort of disappointed that he felt he had to lie to me.

We sometimes choose people who are going to let us down, Ann. There's one in every twelve, at least.

Love Your Neighbor

Seems I'm always asking for stuff *from* you, Jesus, but tell me, how can *I* serve *you*?

I'm thrilled that you asked that, Carl.

How about you love your neighbor as yourself?

OK, but when you say "neighbor," are you talking about the people on my street, or people in Canada, Mexico and the Caribbean?

Yes.

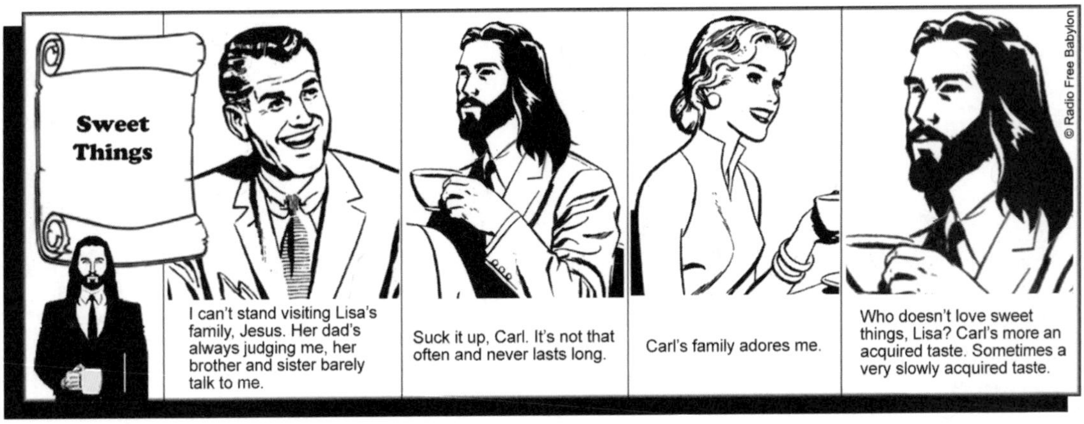
Sweet Things
I can't stand visiting Lisa's family, Jesus. Her dad's always judging me, her brother and sister barely talk to me.
Suck it up, Carl. It's not that often and never lasts long.
Carl's family adores me.
Who doesn't love sweet things, Lisa? Carl's more an acquired taste. Sometimes a very slowly acquired taste.
© Radio Free Babylon

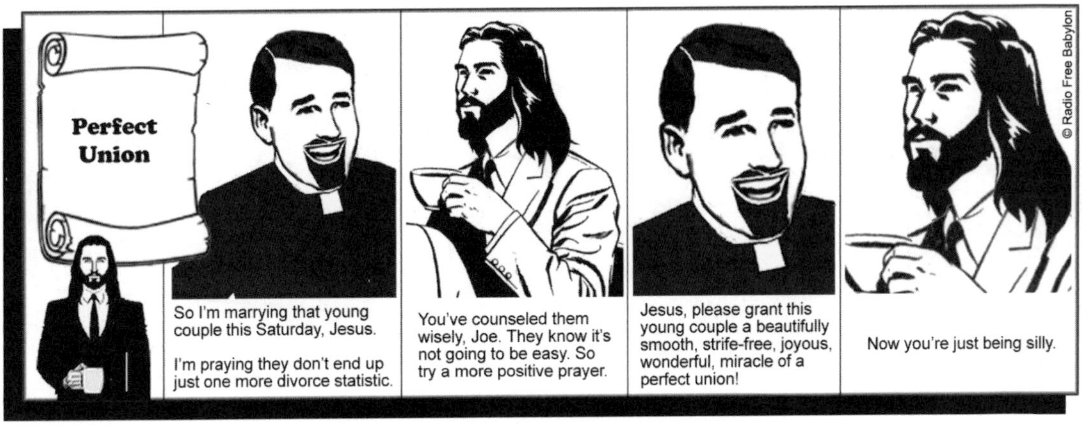
Perfect Union
So I'm marrying that young couple this Saturday, Jesus.
I'm praying they don't end up just one more divorce statistic.
You've counseled them wisely, Joe. They know it's not going to be easy. So try a more positive prayer.
Jesus, please grant this young couple a beautifully smooth, strife-free, joyous, wonderful, miracle of a perfect union!
Now you're just being silly.
© Radio Free Babylon

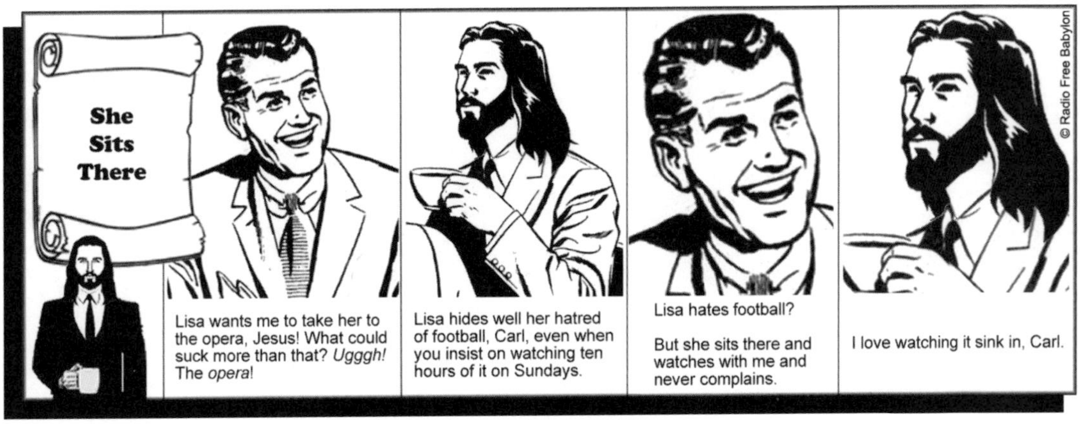
She Sits There
Lisa wants me to take her to the opera, Jesus! What could suck more than that? *Ugggh!* The *opera*!
Lisa hides well her hatred of football, Carl, even when you insist on watching ten hours of it on Sundays.
Lisa hates football?
But she sits there and watches with me and never complains.
I love watching it sink in, Carl.
© Radio Free Babylon

Dinner Tonight

I don't know what got into Carl, but he didn't do his usual Victoria's Secret gift today. He gave me flowers and he says we're going to dinner tonight.

That's exciting, Lisa. You know, despite his clumsy missteps and frequent lapses into stupidity, Carl means the best for you.

Something tells me that you and he have spoken.

Thank you, Jesus.

No biggee. But when he whips out the two-for-one coupon to Applebee's tonight, tell him Jesus said, "Don't be a punk."

Not Your Type

These guys from church want me to be a part of their weekly breakfast thing, Jesus, and I don't know... just not my thing, I guess. Don't really have time.

Not your type of guys, Kevin?

Totally not.

That's why you're going.

Get Along

You know that woman who works with me, the one I've tried so hard to get along with?

Yep. And I notice that the two of you still have a very contentious relationship.

I'd like to ask you to please bless her health, her finances, her family...and even her stupid cats she talks about all the time.

Wow, Ann. You've come a long way from, "Please kill her, Jesus."

I'll get right on this.

ANN

Occupation: Regional Manager
for a nationwide retail chain
Age: 34
Marital Status: Single/Divorced

With two children in middle school, a busy career and an active social life, Ann is strung out and stressed. She looks forward to her coffee with Jesus because, in her words, "He always gets me." She knows she can let her guard all the way down. She's been coming to him daily since she was a child of twelve. Her faith has been a walk of honest questioning, outright complaining and gradual growth.

Politically, Ann leans to the right—sometimes the extreme right—largely due to the influence of her good friends Lisa and Carl, as well as her ex-husband, Jim, an elder of their conservative church. She met Jim at Bible college and promptly married, because sex before marriage is wrong. (Bible college students get around that by getting married—often too early for their own good. Ann asked Jim to leave after he was discovered having an affair.) Ann's slowly learning that Jesus doesn't always share her views on quite a few topics. Active in her church and in community organizations, Ann is service-minded, but she can't help seeking reward and recognition for her efforts.

Ann goes on dates occasionally, often for the wrong reasons, and usually with the wrong men. Past hurts have created in her a bitterness that she's conscious of and actively working through. She's hoping to find a guy who, in her words, "gets me."

4

Sown Among Thorns

Culture

At Radio Free Babylon we have a saying: "Be a Resistor." We explain it like this:

Resisting takes discipline. And when you're being bombarded 24/7 by a culture that encourages indulgence, it'll take some practice.

To "Be a Resistor" is to simply acknowledge how good you have it and maybe take time to appreciate it without wallowing in it excessively. Don't eat when you aren't hungry. Don't watch so much TV. Spend time with family and friends. Turn off your computer. Slow down. You might even try to discreetly and secretly spread that good you have around a little if you want.

"The worries of this life and the deceitfulness of wealth" and the desires for other things can choke the truth (Matthew 13:22). Take advertising copy. I've spent more years than I care to think about writing it. Too much of it is geared toward making people worry over and desire other things, things they don't really need. Bigger. Better. More. I got pretty disgusted with it one day and penned—oh no!—another lyric! Resist this:

SELLER IN THE CELLAR

Sell to win—there is no sin
Grab 'em by the heart—that's the start
Grab 'em by the ears—prey on their fears
Get into their soul—get a hold

You're fat, you're ugly, you're nowhere near sexy
You're old, you're dying, you're sick inside
You're a loser, you're bald, you're lacking something real
and you're just plain stupid if you turn down this deal

Hear that cha-ching?—the register rings
Quota was made—we play in the shade
Palms are greased—space is leased
The clients sing—sales is the thing

You're dumb, you're lacking, your husband doesn't love you
You're slow, you're dated, you're a sad excuse
You're worthless, you're uncool, can't you recognize what's real?
We thought you were smarter when we offered this deal

Fine print is small—don't read it all
It says what it must—as if you can't trust
Would I lie to you? Would I tell you untrue?
If I can get in—give it just the right spin
I sell apples to Eve—and make her believe

that she's a failure, a victim, she needs her eyes opened
Her man's a has-been, substandard, and lacking in size
She's wrinkled, small-breasted, bad mother, lover, wife
until she buys the thing to revolutionize her life

You're a mark, a pigeon, a sucker, easy target
You're insecure, unsure and afraid of the truth
You're a dummy, firm believer, an always-open wallet
You'd sell your body, your soul, or whatever you call it

The shouts from the TV, the calls from the billboards, the rants from the talking heads, the sophomoric soliloquies from celebrity pseudointellectuals, the *unceasing noise* masquerading as truth—resist it if you can. In other words, "When in Rome, *don't* do as the Romans do." (And try not to slap a "Christian" label on a Roman practice and call it good.*)

---

*Disclosure: Our dog's name is Roman.

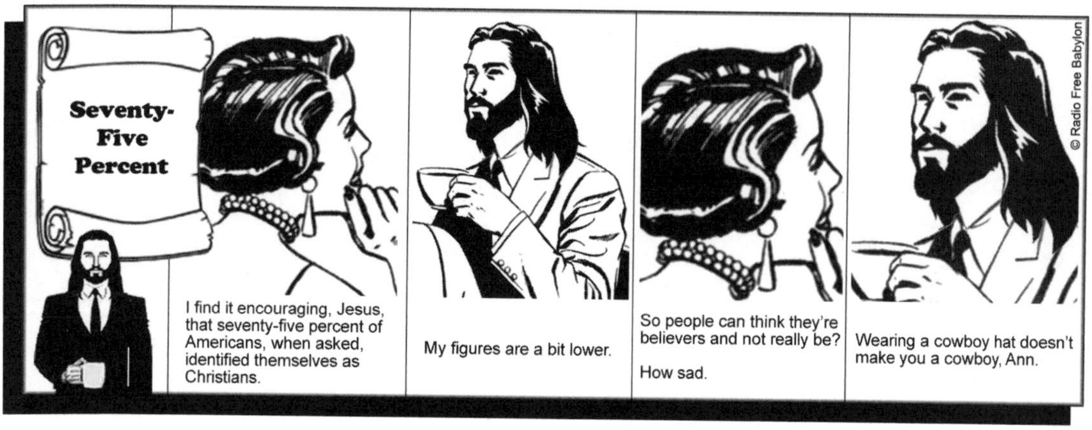
Seventy-Five Percent
I find it encouraging, Jesus, that seventy-five percent of Americans, when asked, identified themselves as Christians.
My figures are a bit lower.
So people can think they're believers and not really be?
How sad.
Wearing a cowboy hat doesn't make you a cowboy, Ann.
© Radio Free Babylon

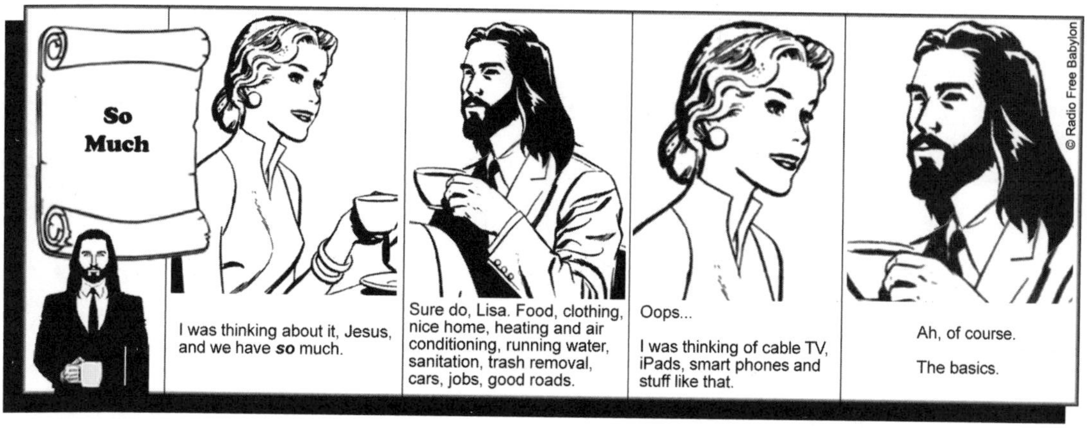
So Much
I was thinking about it, Jesus, and we have *so* much.
Sure do, Lisa. Food, clothing, nice home, heating and air conditioning, running water, sanitation, trash removal, cars, jobs, good roads.
Oops...
I was thinking of cable TV, iPads, smart phones and stuff like that.
Ah, of course.
The basics.
© Radio Free Babylon

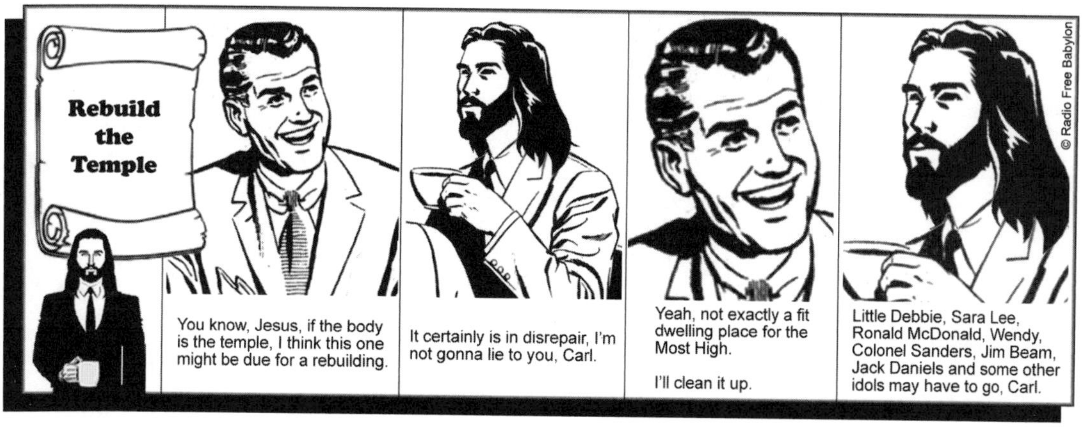
Rebuild the Temple
You know, Jesus, if the body is the temple, I think this one might be due for a rebuilding.
It certainly is in disrepair, I'm not gonna lie to you, Carl.
Yeah, not exactly a fit dwelling place for the Most High.
I'll clean it up.
Little Debbie, Sara Lee, Ronald McDonald, Wendy, Colonel Sanders, Jim Beam, Jack Daniels and some other idols may have to go, Carl.
© Radio Free Babylon

Complete Opposite End

It's weird, Jesus, but I just met some followers of yours who are on the *complete opposite end* of the political spectrum from me.

GASP!

Very funny, Jesus...but, I just don't see how they can reconcile their faith with their position on...

I'll handle the reconciling, Ann. Your job is to love them...or... maybe just not hate them.

Baby steps.

Favorite Christian Singer

Who's your favorite Christian singer, Jesus?

One of my favorites is a woman from a small village in northern Thailand. Sings her heart out all day long while farming.

Oh.

So no one anyone's ever heard of.

She won't be touring the church circuit anytime soon, Carl, but she's famous where I come from.

Come the Apocalypse

Come the apocalypse, I'm not too worried. Carl has it all figured out. We have plenty of water, survival food, medicine, and best of all—gold!

Gold isn't going to be of much value when people are killing each other for a piece of squirrel meat, Lisa.

Oh, gross! *Squirrel meat?* I'm glad we have all those MREs. My favorite one is cheese tortellini in tomato sauce.

Well, *bon appétit*, Lisa!

And Happy Apocalypse!

Some Trust in Chariots

These people who want to cut defense spending, they're so naïve.

Some trust in chariots, Kevin, and some in horses.

Please, this is the real world, Jesus. You can't expect the writings of an ancient king of Israel to be relevant today.

You're right. Let me rephrase:

Some trust in predator drones, Kevin, and some in night vision goggles.

Crossroads

A friend gave me a book that is just frightening. It's about our culture being at a crossroads and the ten things we must do to get on the right path.

Variations of that book have been regurgitated for forty years. It's a popular theme and an easy sell for some publishers.

Perhaps because it's *needed*? People should be warned of the dangers we face if we continue down this path!

The "crossroads" are long behind you, Ann, and it's a one-way street. Covered in ice. And your brakes are shot. And the accelerator is stuck.

Render Unto Caesar

You know that time when those dudes asked you, "Is it right to pay taxes to Caesar?" and you said, "Bring me a coin and tell me whose picture is on it"?

Sure, Carl. And I told them to give to Caesar what is his, and to God the things that are God's. Stumped 'em good that day.

Yeah, well I got a pocketful of hundred dollar bills with Ben Franklin's picture on them, and that old dude is nowhere to be found!

And if I had a nickel for every time I've heard that one, I could build...I dunno...like a big giant nickel house or something.

© Radio Free Babylon

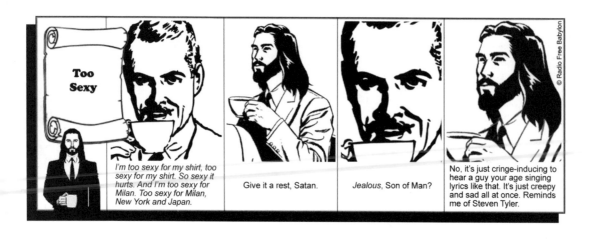

Too Sexy

I'm too sexy for my shirt, too sexy for my shirt. So sexy it hurts. And I'm too sexy for Milan. Too sexy for Milan, New York and Japan.

Give it a rest, Satan.

Jealous, Son of Man?

No, it's just cringe-inducing to hear a guy your age singing lyrics like that. It's just creepy and sad all at once. Reminds me of Steven Tyler.

© Radio Free Babylon

My Cubicle

That part that says, *"and I will dwell in the house of the Lord forever"* sounds a little—how do I put this nicely?—a little confining, Jesus.

It's not a prison, Ann. You're going to love it, trust me.

Will I have a view?

I mean, it's not like my cubicle at work, is it?

That would be hell, Ann.

© Radio Free Babylon

T.G.I.F.

Thank God it's Friday!

The one day I can be sure people who don't normally think of me will.

You know how it is, Jesus. Everybody's working for the weekend.

I really didn't need that song stuck in my head, Carl.

© Radio Free Babylon

Training

I'm training for a triathalon, Jesus. Training, training, training. I've been training so hard. Just training, and more training and training.

I've noticed. You're pretty consumed by it. It's all you talk, tweet and update your Facebook about, Kevin.

That's because training for a triathalon takes tough discipline, and I'm proud of the effort I'm putting into all this training and training.

You know what else takes training and tough discipline? Keeping your mouth shut about how hard you work at being tough and disciplined.

Cute and All

I've decided to expand, Jesus. Hired a couple of guys, bought some more gear, rebranded the company and reserved a good domain name.

Got a suggestion for you: for every ten lawns you mow, mow one more for some poor widow or a sick person at no charge.

A marketing gimmick like that is cute and all, Jesus, but that'd cut into my profit. The margins are pretty slim in this business.

Giving is only a gimmick if you start marketing it, Carl.

It's Your Name

The frequency with which your name is abused on TV is just shocking, Jesus. They say "Christ" and "Jesus" all the time!

My name has always been abused, Lisa. That the abuse should find its way to TV is just a sign of the times.

Well, it's cheap and it shows a lack of creativity.

It's not a swear word! It's your *name*!

And it is no less powerful.

Guess who people think of every time they hear it?

Coming and Going

Permits, licenses, fees, taxes. It's hard out there for a small businessman, Jesus! They get you coming and going!

Yeah, we paid some heavy taxes at Joseph & Son Carpentry Shop, too.

Why didn't you just vote out the big government types and elect some leaders who were more business friendly?

Ha! Vote!

Good one, Carl.

Small Business

It must've been so simple to operate a small business back in your day, Jesus.

Pretty much. You learned a trade from your dad and then took over the business when he got too old.

Yeah, but no silly human resources regulations. No crazy health insurance mandate. No impossibly complicated tax codes.

Yeah, taxes were simple. A guy showed up with a sword, demanded to see your books, then took what he wanted. Ah...the good ol' days.

The Last Days

I know that people of every generation have thought they were living in the End Times, Jesus, but I think we *really* are.

It's true. Every generation has been absolutely *certain* that they were the ones who would witness the last days.

I guess I need to be more direct. Are we living in the last days, Jesus?

Allow me to be direct as well, Lisa; you don't get to know, so quit asking.

© Radio Free Babylon

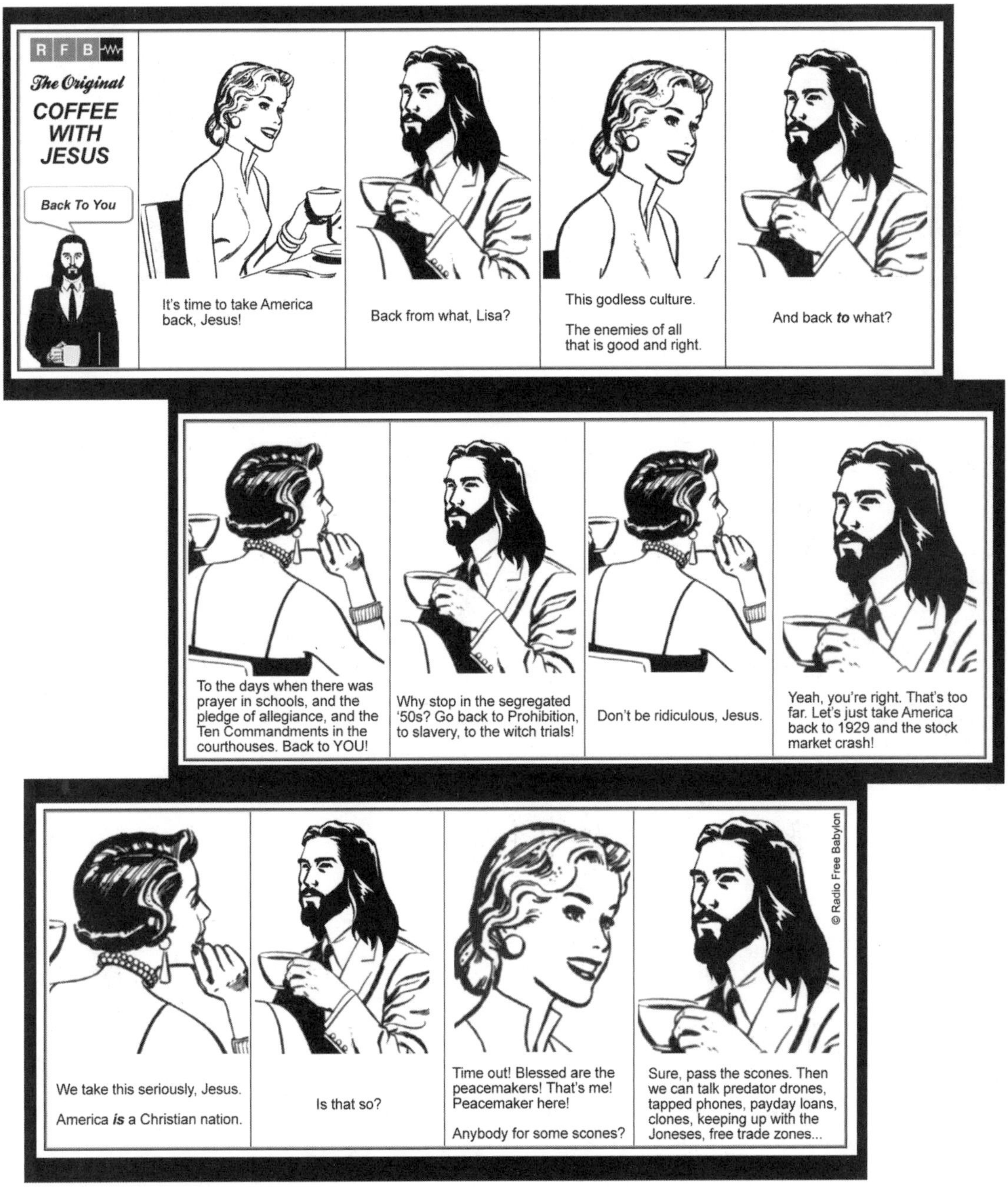
R F B
The Original
COFFEE WITH JESUS
Back To You
It's time to take America back, Jesus!
Back from what, Lisa?
This godless culture.
The enemies of all that is good and right.
And back *to* what?
To the days when there was prayer in schools, and the pledge of allegiance, and the Ten Commandments in the courthouses. Back to YOU!
Why stop in the segregated '50s? Go back to Prohibition, to slavery, to the witch trials!
Don't be ridiculous, Jesus.
Yeah, you're right. That's too far. Let's just take America back to 1929 and the stock market crash!
We take this seriously, Jesus.
America *is* a Christian nation.
Is that so?
Time out! Blessed are the peacemakers! That's me! Peacemaker here!
Anybody for some scones?
Sure, pass the scones. Then we can talk predator drones, tapped phones, payday loans, clones, keeping up with the Joneses, free trade zones...
© Radio Free Babylon

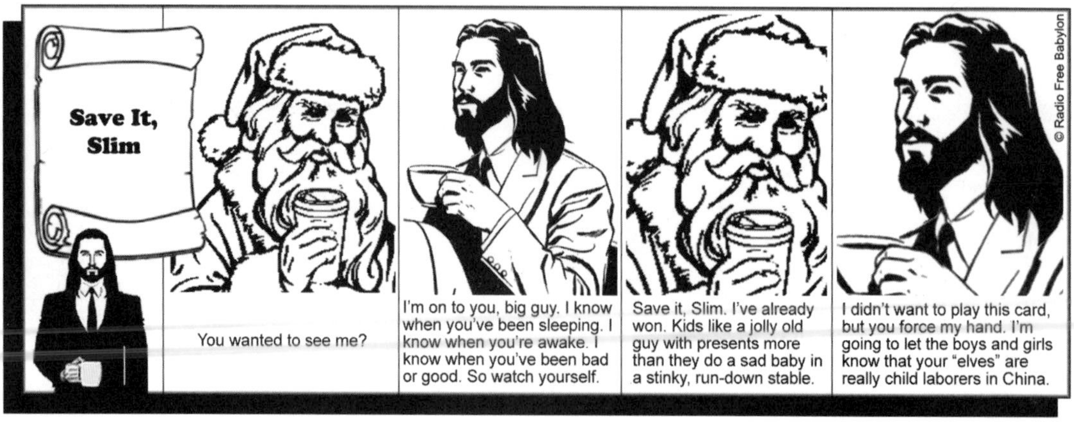
Save It, Slim
You wanted to see me?
I'm on to you, big guy. I know when you've been sleeping. I know when you're awake. I know when you've been bad or good. So watch yourself.
Save it, Slim. I've already won. Kids like a jolly old guy with presents more than they do a sad baby in a stinky, run-down stable.
I didn't want to play this card, but you force my hand. I'm going to let the boys and girls know that your "elves" are really child laborers in China.
© Radio Free Babylon

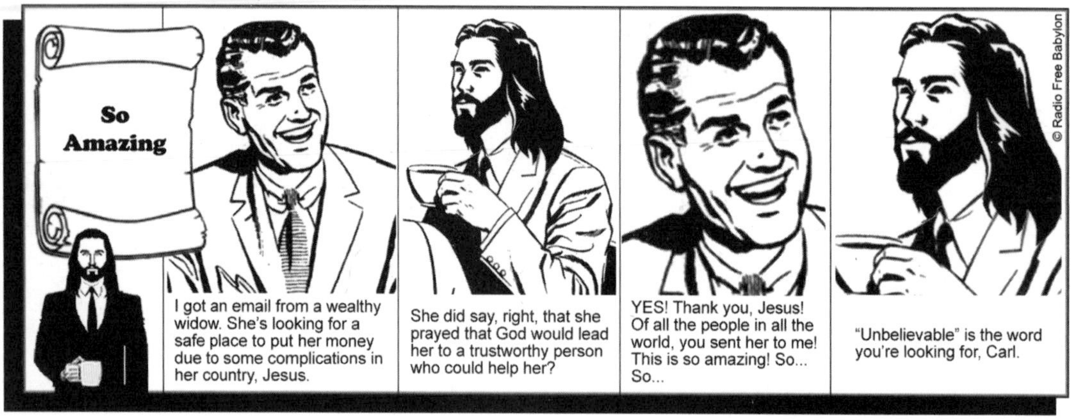
So Amazing
I got an email from a wealthy widow. She's looking for a safe place to put her money due to some complications in her country, Jesus.
She did say, right, that she prayed that God would lead her to a trustworthy person who could help her?
YES! Thank you, Jesus! Of all the people in all the world, you sent her to me! This is so amazing! So... So...
"Unbelievable" is the word you're looking for, Carl.
© Radio Free Babylon

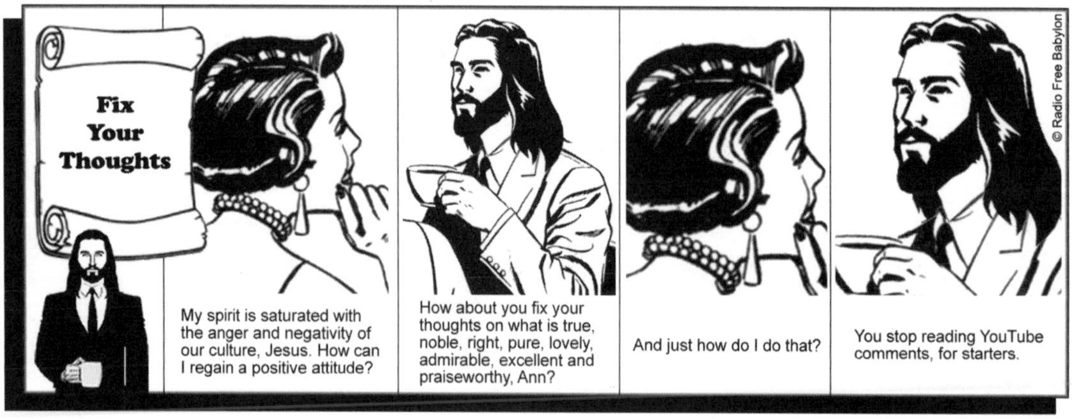
Fix Your Thoughts
My spirit is saturated with the anger and negativity of our culture, Jesus. How can I regain a positive attitude?
How about you fix your thoughts on what is true, noble, right, pure, lovely, admirable, excellent and praiseworthy, Ann?
And just how do I do that?
You stop reading YouTube comments, for starters.
© Radio Free Babylon

Making a Scene

My favorite part in the Bible is when you go into the temple and start dumping tables and whipping the money changers and dove dealers.

I was making a point, Carl. And as a disclaimer, no animals were harmed during the making of that scene.

It was classic! Country carpenter arrives in the big city, starts setting things right and kickin' butt! You were like Clint Eastwood!

You have that backwards. If you take a closer look at Eastwood's body of work, you can see the guy has a real messiah complex.

© Radio Free Babylon

Attractive, Not Repellent

I've organized an online petition and a bunch of us are going to picket the state house to make certain our voices are heard, Jesus.

Do me a favor this time and try to be attractive, not repellent, Kevin.

This issue is important to us, Jesus! Sometimes we get a little fired up.

If you're going to act like an ass, though, keep my name off your signs.

And spell-check them.

© Radio Free Babylon

Kitchen Remodeled

I was so hoping we could afford to have our kitchen remodeled. As it stands, it's just too embarrassing to entertain company.

Oh, I know what *that* means. "Be thankful you even *have* a kitchen, Lisa. It'd be the envy of three quarters of the world."

I like that you're learning to know my thoughts, Lisa.

© Radio Free Babylon

Something Real

Too bad there were no camera phones back in your day, Jesus.

That'd show all the skeptics and naysayers.

Not likely, Carl.

Skepticism is alive and well on YouTube.

But then we'd have proof of your life and resurrection.

We could show people something real.

I was kinda counting on you to show people something real, Carl.

Total Troll

I joined another one of those online Bible discussion groups, Son of Man. It's such *delicious fun*, messing with your silly, sleepy sheep.

Tossing in red herrings?

Sowing seeds of doubt?

Being a total troll, Satan?

Just doing my job, boy king.

Awesome. Because many are now reexamining the twisted, half-baked doctrines you've been whispering in their ears all these years.

Many Are Called

I'm having a hard time with this verse, Jesus: *"Many are called, but few are chosen."*

You have to make a lot of calls sometimes, Carl, before you get to that one person willing to listen.

OK, I get it now! It's like when I worked in that call center selling timeshares!

Yeah...no. You were offering a week a year in Orlando for twenty-five grand. Pretty easy to hang up on that. This is eternity in paradise for free.

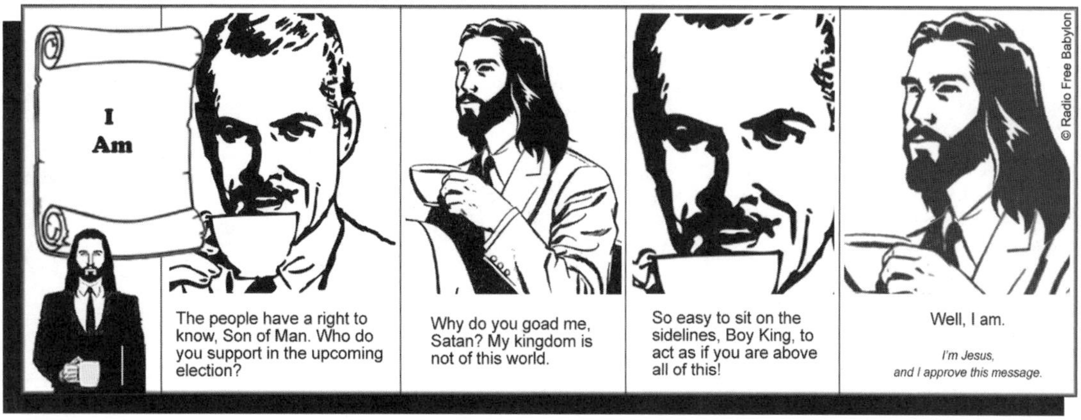
I Am
The people have a right to know, Son of Man. Who do you support in the upcoming election?
Why do you goad me, Satan? My kingdom is not of this world.
So easy to sit on the sidelines, Boy King, to act as if you are above all of this!
Well, I am.
I'm Jesus, and I approve this message.
© Radio Free Babylon

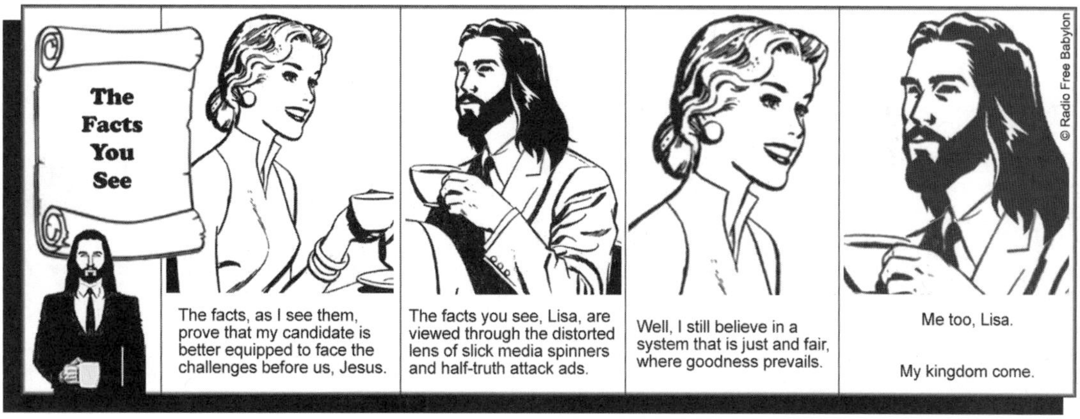
The Facts You See
The facts, as I see them, prove that my candidate is better equipped to face the challenges before us, Jesus.
The facts you see, Lisa, are viewed through the distorted lens of slick media spinners and half-truth attack ads.
Well, I still believe in a system that is just and fair, where goodness prevails.
Me too, Lisa.
My kingdom come.
© Radio Free Babylon

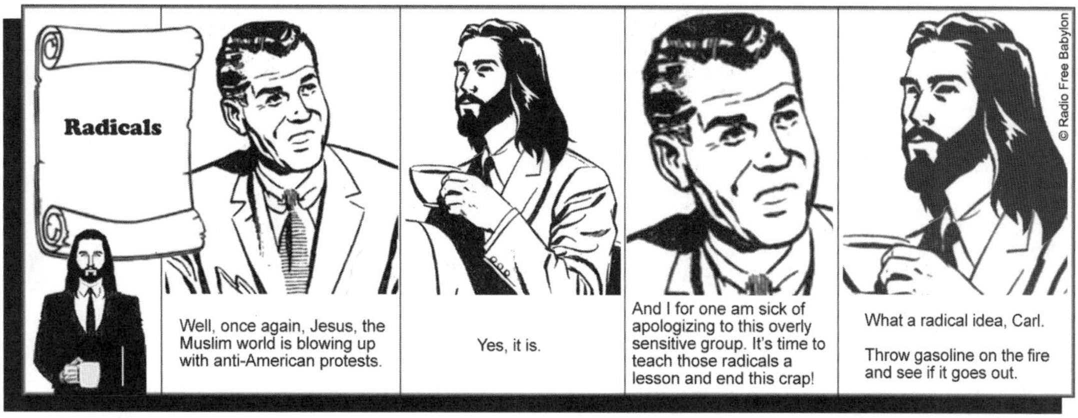
Radicals
Well, once again, Jesus, the Muslim world is blowing up with anti-American protests.
Yes, it is.
And I for one am sick of apologizing to this overly sensitive group. It's time to teach those radicals a lesson and end this crap!
What a radical idea, Carl.
Throw gasoline on the fire and see if it goes out.
© Radio Free Babylon

Barely Speak English

So I'm at the 7-Eleven gassing up the mowers and getting my snacks, and the new clerk can barely speak English. He's all, "Dat vil be tirty-seben tirty-bibe."

And how many languages can you speak, Carl?

Class dismissed.

What a Shame

This car goes racing past me on the highway, swerving from lane to lane—and get this! It had a bumper sticker for the local Christian radio station!

What a shame.

No joke! If you're gonna support that vapid station by displaying their sticker, you should maybe drive with some courtesy.

Sorry, Kevin. I meant it's a shame that you spend your day looking for people to judge so you can feel better about yourself.

We're Still Here

Wow! We're still *here*!

That End of the World thing wasn't real after all!

All that worry for nothing.

Man, I feel kinda stupid now.

The way you behaved at that End of the World party last night is why you should feel stupid, Carl. But yeah, glad *that's* behind us!

Hey, guys. Over here.

LISA

Occupation: Stay-at-home mom
Age: 40
Marital Status: Married

Lisa is an optimist—a sunny, beautiful ("Thank you, Doctor Steve!") optimist. Accustomed to the finer things in life, this happy and helpful woman grew up the youngest child of a doting, upper middle-class Christian couple. She can't remember a time when Jesus and country clubs weren't a part of her life. An excellent student, cheer captain and homecoming queen, Lisa went on to college where she met a smooth-talking, handsome jock named Carl. They were married in her sophomore year—not by choice.

Spa vacations, personal trainers, nice cars, fine food and drink are what Lisa expects, but she is not unappreciative of these things. She has unfathomable patience with her husband, the gregarious (and notorious) Carl, whose frequent lapses in judgment often land the family in financial jeopardy.

Now that their youngest child is in elementary school, Lisa is eager to finally put her Communications degree to work, hoping she's still pretty enough to break into broadcast journalism.

When she isn't wearing rose-colored glasses, Lisa can be found wearing blinders. Jesus often removes them for her.

5

This Against You

Church

They come in as many shapes, sizes and personalities as the people who belong to them, and like the people, none of them are perfect. And in a comic, they're going to be ridiculously imperfect.

"The church may stink, but it's the best thing afloat," a pastor once told me, quoting another pastor who was quoting another pastor who was quoting an author who had plagiarized another author who had paraphrased another. Having served in a few in varying leadership roles, I found that church work really is *work*, with all the politics, jockeying and glad-handing found in most office settings. A handful of people do most of the work, and gossip is a favorite pastime. But you'll also find some of the best people you'll ever get to know within a church. They're usually really old. They got wise. And very rare is the church where a visitor would feel unwelcome.

Stand in the foyer of most churches on a Sunday morning and you'll see happy faces, and everyone's response to everyone's query is, "Great! How about you?" (and they're of course great and fine as well).

We tend to wear masks. We're often there for a show, well rehearsed, executed flawlessly and on time so that the next performance can start on schedule. Sitting in those pews, or those stackable chairs, or those plush balcony seats with cup-holder armrests, are people who aren't fine. They're not great. They're struggling. They hurt. Maybe they fought on the way to church. Maybe they just wanted to stay in their pajamas and be with their kids on this day off, but they got dressed and ready and shuffled the kids off to their various classrooms so they could color a picture of Jesus. Hopefully they'll get something out of being among their brothers and sisters.

Maybe it's OK to take a day off every now and then from what has become "church" in this society. Maybe a three-point sermon delivered within the allotted time by a person at a lectern with a theology degree isn't always the best way to discover the nature and character of God.

Most pastors would agree with that last statement. It's the ones that don't that we'll have fun with in this section.

In Thine Eyes

Thou knowest, O Lord, that thy servant doth strive to do thy will, to be pleasing in thine eyes. And yea, steadfastly do I seek thy loving-kindness.

Ann, knock it off.

What dost thou desire that thy servant "knock off," O Lord?

Talking to me in a voice other than "thine own," Ann.

Cool New Logos

My firm assists churches with electronic ministry, among other things. We get them updated, helping them to reach out more effectively.

So, you're the ones creating the cool new church logos and the clever ad campaigns.

Yep! We also design social media strategies, email ministry platforms, even interior design and staff wardrobe suggestions!

I call this the "Panera Bread" church. I look forward to the day when your churches meet in secret. You have no idea what you're missing.

Shake Things Up

I need to do something to shake things up, so I'm going to start a sermon series called, *"God's Plan for a Happy Sex Life."* Whaddaya think, Jesus?

Been done. Gimmicky way to draw attention to your church, Joe. Save it for counseling sessions or small groups.

It's an issue we should talk about! *AND!* I'll challenge all married couples to have sex every night for a week!

Guaranteed to disgust their children, Joe.

Think of *the children*, Joe!

Called

I think I'm being called to the ministry, Jesus.

Might wanna check caller ID on that one, Carl, 'cause I'm pretty sure it wasn't me.

I think I'd make a great megachurch senior pastor. Or a hugely successful Christian recording artist.

Yeah, who wouldn't be able to do those things?

But you said ministry.

Unexplained Things

If you still performed miracles today, there'd be a show on Discovery Channel dedicated to trying to debunk them.

And each episode would end with that ambiguous closing line they use for all shows about unexplained things: *"We may never know!"*

Ha! So true, Jesus!

So...*ummm*...how come you don't perform miracles anymore?

Oh, I do, Lisa. I just don't perform them where I'm not expected to.

Like at your church.

Slap a Cross On It

We're developing a line of Christian clothing for today's youth. It's a way for them to express their faith without sacrificing style or design.

If there's one thing my people are good at, it's taking a trendy, popular thing, slapping a cross on it and calling it "Christian."

That reminds me! We're developing a series of young adult novels based on a Christian vampire character. Sexy but safe.

You're a real forward thinker, Kevin. I fully expect you to be a pioneer of the Christian porn industry.

© Radio Free Babylon

Without a Vision

Part One

I'm going to present to the church board my vision for expansion, Jesus.

But your church is nowhere near full, Joe. There's no need to expand at this point.

That's where the "vision" part comes in, boss! You know, *"Without a vision, the people perish,"* right?

Or is this a case of *"Without Joe's vision, the people move on to the cooler church down the road?"*

Relevant

There's a new church starting up in town that promises to be "relevant" and different.

Think I might try it.

You keep searching for the perfect church, Carl, but you're never going to find it.

Then maybe this is a sign that I need to start *my own* church!

The Church of Carl!

Which would fast become a cult, Carl.

No, this is a sign that *you* need to be relevant.

Pancake Breakfast

The monthly pancake breakfast at church used to be such a hit. Now it's just a few old timers and a couple of homeless guys.

People probably prefer a gluten-free rice flour option.

Maybe we could raffle off a scooter? And get some moody, acoustic duo to play? Or, I know! Karaoke and craft beer!

Or, I know! You could look at the pancake breakfast as a ministry to old timers and homeless guys!

Consumer

We've identified the key desires of the consumer, prioritizing them into an action plan that we'll take to the church board to approve for implementation.

Fascinating stuff, Kevin. So the "consumer" in your study is the potential churchgoer?

More precisely, he or she is the *disaffected* potential churchgoer, Jesus, with a median income between 100 and 150 thousand.

It's a tough church market, isn't it? You're going to need some attractive incentives to build brand loyalty. How about valet parking? Or VIP seating?

Great Seats

We got great seats in the mezzanine yesterday at church, with an unobstructed view of the big screens near the stage, Jesus.

By "stage," I think you mean altar, Lisa. Well, good for you. I suppose you had to get there early for such a great worship experience.

Yeah, about an hour early, but we grabbed scones and coffees in the foyer, then settled in and waited for the show. I mean the service.

Was there an encore? And were you able to get a picture or an autograph from the pastor after the show?

Picture of Me

I have to substitute teach the third-grade Sunday school class this morning. Those little monsters make me want to scream.

Twenty kids freshly filled with sugary cereal all crammed in a small room and told to color a picture of me. Sucks for them too, Ann.

We do what we can do, Jesus, with the things we have. Do you have any better suggestions?

Try to adjust your attitude some so that fewer of them are telling their parents on the way home, "We had the mean teacher today."

© Radio Free Babylon

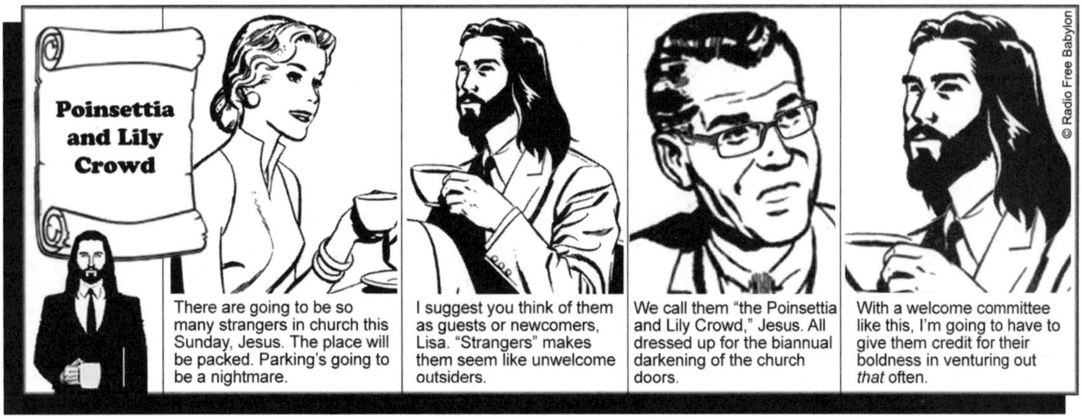
Poinsettia and Lily Crowd
There are going to be so many strangers in church this Sunday, Jesus. The place will be packed. Parking's going to be a nightmare.
I suggest you think of them as guests or newcomers, Lisa. "Strangers" makes them seem like unwelcome outsiders.
We call them "the Poinsettia and Lily Crowd," Jesus. All dressed up for the biannual darkening of the church doors.
With a welcome committee like this, I'm going to have to give them credit for their boldness in venturing out *that* often.
© Radio Free Babylon

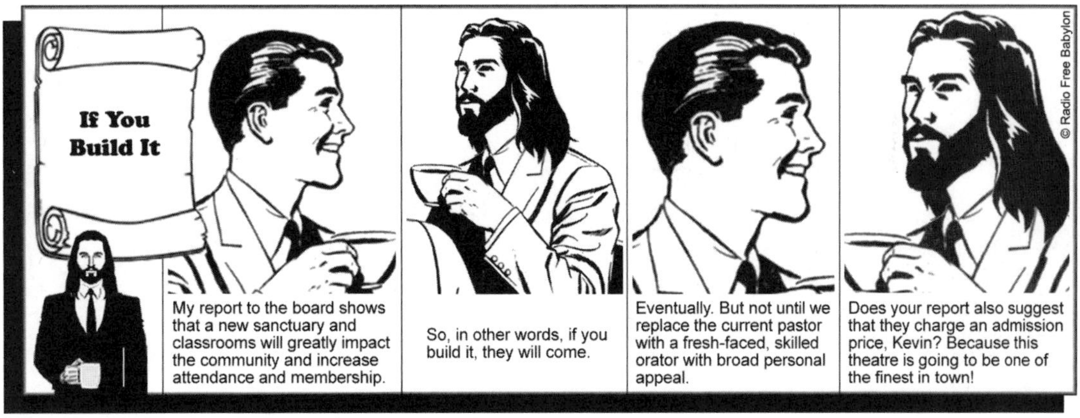
If You Build It
My report to the board shows that a new sanctuary and classrooms will greatly impact the community and increase attendance and membership.
So, in other words, if you build it, they will come.
Eventually. But not until we replace the current pastor with a fresh-faced, skilled orator with broad personal appeal.
Does your report also suggest that they charge an admission price, Kevin? Because this theatre is going to be one of the finest in town!
© Radio Free Babylon

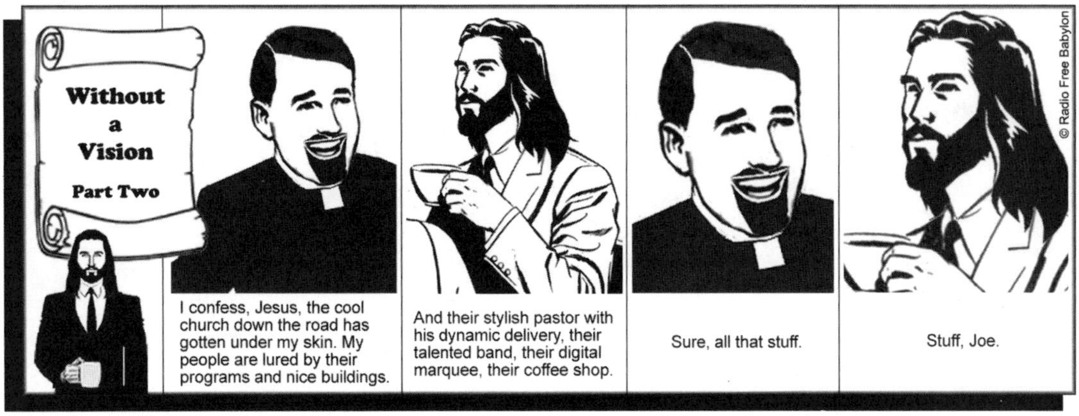
Without a Vision
Part Two
I confess, Jesus, the cool church down the road has gotten under my skin. My people are lured by their programs and nice buildings.
And their stylish pastor with his dynamic delivery, their talented band, their digital marquee, their coffee shop.
Sure, all that stuff.
Stuff, Joe.
© Radio Free Babylon

Uncool

We've tried multiple ways over the years to make following you seem cool, Jesus, but the kids just aren't buying that notion.

Yeah, by most standards, Kevin, following me is pretty uncool, no matter how you package it or dress it up in hip attitudes.

Maybe we just need to go with *that*!

We'll make uncool the *new cool*!

Or! Ditch the idea that I'm the leader of a clique with its own music and dress code, Kevin.

Can't Schedule Revival

The Pentecostal church's marquee says they're having a revival Sunday through Wednesday of next week, Jesus.

I'll be there, Carl, but you know you can't schedule revival.

But the evangelist they booked is renowned for his anointed preaching and healing ministry, Jesus.

Movements of the Spirit will not be announced by church marquee, Lisa.

When It Matters

A doctrinal difference here, a theological quibble there, and I can have your people arguing like the worst of enemies, Son of Man.

They'll agree on the basics, Satan, when it really matters.

The *basics*? They can barely agree on your *name*!

I divide, then I subtract. It's quite simple, really.

And I will continue to add and multiply.

Do the math, loser.

The Original
COFFEE WITH JESUS

Great Churches

I think it's great that you're looking to expand the vision of your church, Joe. This town has plenty of room for more great churches.

But we aren't looking to move to a new church.

Not yet, anyway.

I wasn't asking you to, Carl. I understand you and Lisa are very happy over at Worship World.

I remember when Worship World was just a few families. Now it's thousands. Someday your church will get there, Joe.

Not really my goal, Ann. I'm just trying to keep it alive.

You should visit with Pastor Steve over at Worship World. I'm sure he'd give you a few tips. I can put in a word for you.

I know Steve. We have a monthly breakfast with all the other local pastors.

Oh? I wasn't aware of this clergy confab.

It sounds dangerously... ecumenical.

More like New Age!

Who started this "unity breakfast" of yours?

I did, Carl.

Yeah, it was his idea.

Let's switch it to weekly and really give 'em a scare, Joe.

© Radio Free Babylon

Revelations

Our women's group is going through Revelations and we're having an awfully hard time figuring out some of the symbolism. Scary, much of it.

It's the Book of *Revelation*, not "Revelations." *For the last time, it's singular!* Anyway, sorry—pet peeve. You were saying, Ann?

Ann is obsessed with the identity of the Antichrist and she's wondering if you could give us a hint. He's a Jew, right? From Europe?

A few years ago you were convinced he was a Muslim from Hawaii by way of Kansas and Kenya. Maybe you should switch to John's Gospel.

Crazy on Fire

You ever notice how much time some atheists devote to talking about something they don't believe in?

Some of them are regular zealots, crazy on fire about their beliefs. Or their non-beliefs. Whatever.

They're relentless! They're crusaders! They simply won't rest until they've convinced you that they're right! So off-putting!

You're onto something here, Carl. Perhaps self-righteous, cocky anger is not the most effective tool for evangelism.

Misleading Others

That guy predicting the date of the rapture! What a joke!

It's easy to make fun, but try to leave the old man alone, Kevin.

He's ninety, for My sake!

But he's the one out there making public promises in your name, misleading others!

Yeah, and you once said, "till death do us part" in front of a church full of people and me too. How'd that work out for ya, slick?

© Radio Free Babylon

Mission Trip

I'm going to be a chaperone on the youth group's mission trip to Orlando, Jesus. They'll help an underserved church in a poor part of town.

Wonderful. Painting, roof repair, that sort of thing? Perhaps a little landscaping? Minister to some local kids?

Yeah, that covers Monday and Tuesday, then we'll be free to do Disney, Universal Studios and Sea World until Friday.

Amazing how many churches in tourist destinations need help, isn't it, Carl? I hope you can squeeze in a side trip to the beach.

Rebranding

First we renamed it. Grace Fellowship is now called Rock Church. And I suggested Facebook pages and Twitter accounts for the staff.

The rebranding is complete. And now the people can know what the second assistant middle school pastor had for breakfast.

It's good for the people to know they can reach out to the staff at any time, Jesus. A church should take advantage of these tools.

Seems to me like some tool is taking advantage of these churches, Kevin. Have you recommended cupholders in the sanctuary yet?

Go to Church

There are some Sundays, Jesus, when I just want to sleep in late, stay in my pajamas and enjoy a quiet day alone.

I'm not keeping attendance at your church, Ann.

So I don't *have* to go to church? That almost makes me *want* to go to church!

As you're not a sports fan, this Sunday might be a good one to miss. Your pastor is phoning it in with some football analogy sermon.

© Radio Free Babylon

Where's the Fire?

Whatever happened to my denomination, Jesus? We were pioneers, trailblazers!

Where's the *fire*?

I'm going to sit here quietly while you work this one out, Joe.

Hmmmmmmm...

Ah!...I think I get it...

Starts with me, doesn't it?

Is that a spark I see?

New Worship Leader

I don't like this new worship leader the church brought in, Jesus. He thinks he's a rock star. And his wife! *Ugggh!*

She gets an awful lot of solos, that's for sure.

But she's got a great voice and a sweet heart.

And a ton of hairspray and makeup!

The cameras shouldn't zoom in so close on her.

You won't be suffering long, Ann. This is just a pit stop on their way to Nashville.

In the Army

It was so different in the Army, Jesus. The soldiers *wanted* to talk to the chaplains. Now, it's like, "Hey, Joe. Nice sermon. Bye."

The same needs are still present, Joe.

You'll have to dig a little deeper with this group.

I suppose I could be more available to them, be out in the town, not locked up in my study trying to write next week's killer sermon.

Well? Get on it, soldier.

Report back to me at 18:30 hours.

Super Psyched

This guy from church wants to come by the house to talk with Lisa and me about working with him, Jesus!

And did he say he has a "*management opportunity*" for you in his "*new company*" because "*you seem like a sharp guy,*" Carl?

YES!

I'm super psyched!

Super psyched is just how they want you, Carl. Learn this from the Old Testament:

When you see a pyramid, run.

Piece of Toast

How come people are always finding images of you in the weirdest places, like the side of a cow, a piece of toast, an office-building window?

When you combine fervent faith with wild imaginations, you're going to get some wildly faithful people. But the toast one is just stupid.

And if someone doesn't point it out to you, it's very hard to see. I mean, I thought the toast one looked more like Brad Pitt.

We see what we want to see, Lisa.

Plant and Water

I think my sermon yesterday fell on deaf ears, Jesus.

You have no idea who was reached or what they took from it, Joe. It could be years from now and someone remembers what you said.

But you know I've always wanted to bring in a great harvest for you, Jesus.

You plant and water, Joe.

Let me worry about what grows.

Not Being Fed

I might be making a switch to another church pretty soon, Jesus.

I'm going to ask you why, Kevin, and you're going to give me a straight answer.

I'm just not being *fed*, ya know?...*OK! OK!* Because I've networked this group all I can and I need some fresh leads!

Money changers in the temple had nothing on you, son.

Around One Person

Man, did you see how badly the Saints beat the Colts last weekend? It was like eighty-nine to nothing or some crazy lopsided score.

The lesson there is that you can't build your entire organization around one person. Once he or she is gone, the whole thing falls.

I see what you're getting at. Like those big churches where the pastor is some super speaker and great motivator.

Nah, those guys are a dime a dozen. I was thinking more along the lines of your great frontmen like Jim Morrison or Michael Hutchence.

I Give Up

This church is going to be dead in a decade if something doesn't turn around soon, Jesus.

You don't have any more plans to inject life into it, Joe? No more proven methods from the experts?

I've tried it all, Jesus. I'm totally out of ideas.

I give up.

Finally!

Now we can get to work.

JOE

Occupation: Pastor
Age: 29
Marital Status: Unknown

Joe pastors a small, struggling church in Anytown, USA. (On Main Street, of course.) His denomination, if he even has one, is unknown. He wears a cleric's collar simply so you'll recognize what he is. He might be married, but then you'd draw conclusions that we don't want you to, so that, for now, is also unknown.

What is certain is this: While serving in the Army as a chaplain's assistant, Joe finished school. Upon discharge from service, he went to seminary and was ordained. Now he leads a church. He's new in town, new to the state and new to his congregation. He misses the Army some days. He had dreams—big dreams—of a big church and a big impact, so he sometimes falls prey to the gimmicks and tricks of the church-growth experts as he tries to compete with Worship World, the big church on the edge of town.

Joe takes his work very seriously. He's not afraid to get his hands dirty. (He has no choice. The church can't afford a janitor.) He sometimes gets frustrated.

Joe is always smiling. Oftentimes it's a real smile.

6

The Rain Came Down

Suffering, Temptation and Comfort

Bad things happen. We get dumped. We get fired. We get sick. We fall on our faces, stumbling over a thing we never thought we would.

And here come our friends to tell us that "Everything happens for a reason!" and "God doesn't close one door without opening another!" Perhaps, but here in this dark hallway full of locked doors, that reason isn't clear. (And who said the opening and the closing were simultaneous anyway?)

And here comes the poet: "The times when you have seen only one set of footprints, that is when I carried you." That's nice, but it doesn't explain why my mouth and nose are full of sand.

The rain comes, count on it. The streams rise, always have. The winds blow, guaranteed. Your house washes away or it doesn't.

"Consider it pure joy," James said, "whenever you face trials of many kinds."

I think it's safe to say that James was a pretty rare guy, with a waterproof, windproof house. Most of us aren't there yet.

This section deals with suffering, temptation and hope. And by now you should've expected it. Here's another lyric.

WHILE WE'RE WAITING

While we're waiting, why don't we walk down
We'll watch the waves, whipped by the wind—and the water all around

Touch me talking, taste the trembled fear
Tell the tale—torn from a tree—and the mud made by tears

Direct the daybreak, deal a brand new day
Dial down the darkness—drive the doubt away

COFFEE WITH JESUS

Feel the future, a fate that's formed in love
The facts are faced, filled with faith, float the river far above

While we're waiting, why don't we walk down
We'll watch the waves, whipped by the wind—and the water—
Wow, that's wild—there's water all around

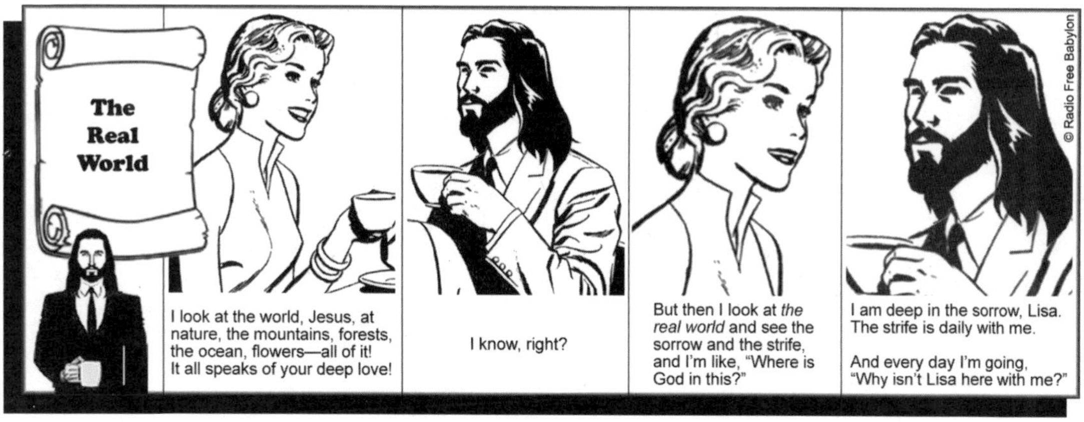
The Real World
I look at the world, Jesus, at nature, the mountains, forests, the ocean, flowers—all of it! It all speaks of your deep love!
I know, right?
But then I look at *the real world* and see the sorrow and the strife, and I'm like, "Where is God in this?"
I am deep in the sorrow, Lisa. The strife is daily with me.
And every day I'm going, "Why isn't Lisa here with me?"
© Radio Free Babylon

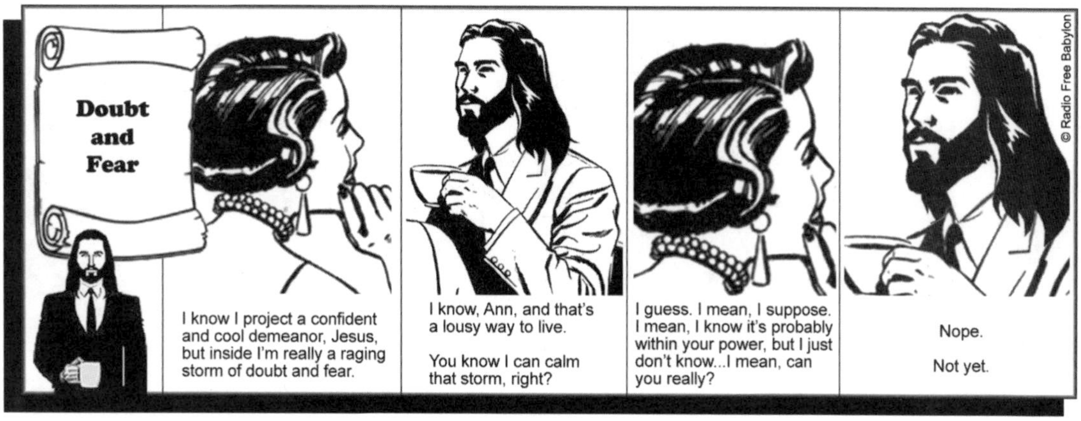
Doubt and Fear
I know I project a confident and cool demeanor, Jesus, but inside I'm really a raging storm of doubt and fear.
I know, Ann, and that's a lousy way to live.
You know I can calm that storm, right?
I guess. I mean, I suppose. I mean, I know it's probably within your power, but I just don't know...I mean, can you really?
Nope.
Not yet.
© Radio Free Babylon

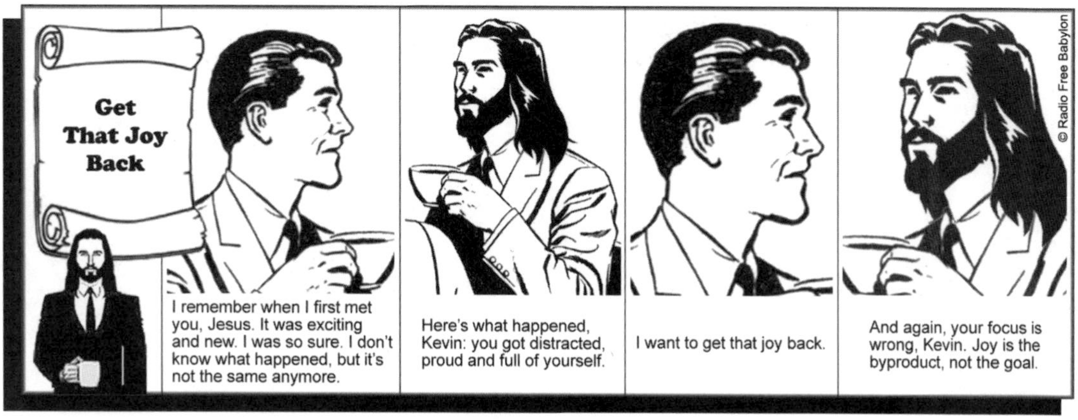
Get That Joy Back
I remember when I first met you, Jesus. It was exciting and new. I was so sure. I don't know what happened, but it's not the same anymore.
Here's what happened, Kevin: you got distracted, proud and full of yourself.
I want to get that joy back.
And again, your focus is wrong, Kevin. Joy is the byproduct, not the goal.
© Radio Free Babylon

Endless Eternal Ecstasy

I've been telling people that Heaven is not only boring, it's a dictatorial place where if you don't bow down and worship, then you're cast out.

You mean if you try to take the throne of God, then you're cast out, Satan.

You're such a liar.

And I've been telling them that *my kingdom* is a place of parties, sex and doing whatever pleases you. Endless, eternal ecstasy!

Liar. Liar.

Pants on...

Never mind.

Swimmer's Body

I'm thinking of getting that surgery that gives you chiseled abs. I'll go from puffy to buff for only about seven thousand dollars.

What a waste, Carl. If you want a swimmer's body, you gotta *swim*! Think of all the better ways to use that money.

Maybe you're right. My hairline could use some restoration, and these crow's feet are definitely not helping my game.

Fine, Carl. Go all out. Don't forget the Porsche and some gold jewelry. But *please* draw the line at V-neck sweaters with nothing underneath.

Your Neighbor's BMW

If looking on a woman with lust is the same as adultery, then Carl is committing adultery a hundred times a day, Jesus.

And how do you categorize the way you look on your neighbor's BMW, Lisa?

That's different. It's just a hunk of metal. A shining, powerful hunk...of... *beautiful* metal. Smooth lines...*lean* and *muscular*.

Snap out of it, Lisa.

All Over Again

If I had it to do all over again, Jesus, I would do so many things differently.

But you *don't* have it to do all over again, Kevin, so why even go there?

But if I only knew then what I know now...

Then you'd have had wisdom beyond your years.

That you didn't earn.

What I Heard

I have it on good authority that a woman in our Sunday School class is separating from her husband. I heard she caught him cheating!

And it wasn't the first time! Well, first time he got caught, anyway. I mean, that's what I heard.

Oh, my! That's just *awful*!

We're praying for them, Jesus.

Uh-huh.

There's a Path

Tell me, Son of Man, why did you make all the things you ask your people *not* to do... so deliciously *fun* to do?

There's a path before each person that *seems* right, but it ends in death, Satan.

You avoid my question, Boy King!

Why did you make the most delightful things forbidden?

As I said, they only *seem* delightful *at first*.

And that was *your* doing, Doctor Deception.

Don't Trust Them

You know those guys standing at the offramp with "Homeless Please Help" or "Will Work for Food" signs? I just don't trust them for some reason, Jesus.

Granted, the offramp is not the ideal place to find work, Carl, but I'm sure they aren't out there making a killing most days.

There are plenty of places where a guy in need can go for help. It smells like a scam to me.

You have twenty-one dollars and sixty-five cents in loose change in your truck's ashtray. Hate to see you scammed out of your Slurpee money, Carl.

That Pacifist Stuff

I think we need to go in and just annihilate Iran. Wipe 'em off the map. They're a threat to peace in the Middle East.

I don't need to point out to you the hypocrisy of that statement, do I, Kevin?

C'mon, Jesus. That pacifist stuff is fine for children, but we live in the real world, with real bad guys and terrorist states.

Do keep in mind, Kevin, that the people being blown up will almost always regard their attackers as terrorists.

Rotten Fruit

Hatred, sadness, discontent, impatience, faithlessness, meanness, coarseness, badness and impulsiveness.

Get to your point, Satan.

My *point*, Son of Man? My point is that *these* are the rotten fruits I have sown among *your* very people!

Yeah well, I'm pretty tight on quality control, so none of those fruits will be loaded on the trucks come harvest time.

God Money Power

Well, Jesus, one more high profile Christian leader has been caught with his pants down.

Fame and money. Power and sex.

I see it all the time.

Looks bad for you, though.

He put himself up on that pedestal, Kevin, not me.

Gouge and Cut

If I'd done as you said and gouged out my eye or cut off my hand when they caused me to sin, Jesus, I'd have been a blind double amputee long ago!

The point, Carl, was that you shouldn't flirt with temptation.

I try not to, but you know, sometimes this leads to that and *boom*, the deed is done.

It's the "this leading to that" part, Carl, where the gouging and cutting need to happen.

Before the *boom*, please.

Minor Celebrity

Some of the women and I are pretty sure that Pastor Dan might be getting a little too friendly with his administrative assistant maybe. Probably.

He *is* a minor celebrity in this town. When you cultivate power and fame, you're going to get all the dangers that come with such things.

I think the turning point was when he promised to get a tattoo if attendance topped five thousand. He's been like a rock star ever since.

The church logo on his bicep was a little much, but so was the Bieber haircut and the Urban Outfitters wardrobe. But hipness, like beauty, fades.

Jesus Is for Losers

I really can't muster up much compassion for people who won't help themselves, Jesus. You know what I'm sayin'?

Compassion, Kevin, comes about by finding a way to simply imagine what it would be like to be in someone else's shoes.

I can imagine it would *suck* to be in those shoes, and so I move on with *my* life, with *my* problems. Who's got time to waste on losers?

Uh...me.

I'm here with you, right?

Consider the Sparrows

My job search has produced absolutely nothing. Maybe I'm trying *too* hard, ya know? I think maybe I just need to "Let go and let God."

If by that you mean you're going to sit at home playing Xbox hoping for a miracle, I'm afraid I can't do much for your job search.

C'mon, Jesus! You're the one who said, "Consider the sparrows," and all that.

The last sparrow I saw sitting on his butt playing *Call of Duty* for six days died of starvation.

So Empty

I'm so empty today, Jesus.

Then please just sip your coffee, Ann.

We don't have to converse.

<sigh>

I hear ya.

RFB

The Original

COFFEE
WITH
JESUS

Talk to ME

Ann, you know what your problem is, don't you? Look at yourself, Ann...such *potential!* This sad, dogmatic Galilean holds you back.

There's a voice in my head sometimes, Jesus, that tries to pull me away from you.

You know what to do with that voice, Ann.

Ann, such a sad, lonely woman you are. You know why that is, don't you, Ann? It's the Nazarene. He makes you sad. Annie, my dearest...

Ann, oh sweet, sweet Ann. The things I can give you! The joys we can and will know together!

Satan! I rebuke you! I rebuke you now in the name of Jesus! And I condemn you to the pit!

Oh, yes! There it is!

Address me, Ann! Talk to ME, Ann! *Pray* to me!

No, Ann. You're in too deep.

Just say, "the Lord rebuke you," like the archangel Michael did.

Oh...sorry.

The Lord rebuke you.

You heard her, Satan.

I rebuke you.

Ick...I think I just threw up a little in my mouth.

I'm out of here.

Next time, Ann, don't let it go that far. You can't walk into the lion's cage and expect not to be devoured.

© Radio Free Babylon

Anxiety

If there is one thing I wish you could fix for me, Jesus, it would be my anxiety.

Here's an idea: find an hour a day when you are free from your iPad, your iPhone, your Netflix, your computer and your 500 TV channels, Lisa.

And I suppose you'll want me to spend that hour in some sort of "quiet reflection," right?

Ding ding ding!

But remember, "reflection" is not the same as "worrying about all the crap in my life."

Fulfill My Destiny

I believe I was put on this earth for a reason, Jesus. I want to fulfill my destiny! I believe you have great things in store for me!

Not everyone is going to be "great," Carl. Some people will walk through life quietly, with dignity, doing my will without being noticed at all.

So are you saying that I'm just going to mow lawns? *That's* my calling in life? *That's* what I was put here to do?

That's what you *get* to do, Carl.

Get Past It

You know that thing I struggle with, Jesus?

I do, Kevin.

I keep asking you to help me get past it, but it's still there, always a temptation.

It's still there because you flirt with it endlessly, love it so much and actively pursue it, Kevin. Put it behind you, not in front of you.

Missing Something

A friend of mine is in the hospital, Jesus. Do I pray for a miracle? For the doctors? For the doctors to witness a miracle? For her healing?

All of that sounds great, Ann.

Wait...I know that tone... I'm missing something, aren't I?

Starts with a "v" and ends with a "t." Rhymes with "miss it."

Acts of Kindness

I'm making an effort to see what I can do for people every day. It's like, if you look around, you can find opportunities to help everywhere.

Sort of the "random act of kindness" idea, huh?

Yeah! It really makes me feel good. I don't know how that works exactly. Just one of those spiritual truths, I guess.

Let's see if you can make it a little more random, Carl, and try to help someone who isn't an attractive female between the ages of 18 and 50.

Tragedy Everywhere

Soldiers shooting children in Afghanistan, neighborhood watch captains shooting unarmed boys in Florida; *what* is going on, Jesus?

You've only named the two most talked about stories in the news, Lisa. I see this stuff every day. There is tragedy everywhere, all the time.

And yet you just sit there! Why do you allow it? Why don't you intervene?

Bold questions from someone who has plenty of opportunities to alleviate the suffering around her. But I believe you're late for a nail appointment, aren't you?

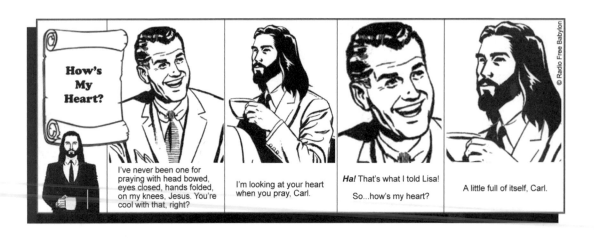

How's My Heart?

I've never been one for praying with head bowed, eyes closed, hands folded, on my knees, Jesus. You're cool with that, right?

I'm looking at your heart when you pray, Carl.

Ha! That's what I told Lisa! So...how's my heart?

A little full of itself, Carl.

Resist

Hey, Lisa. *Psssst!* LISA! Hey! *Liiiiissssssaaaa!* You know you want to do it. C'mon, Lisa! DO IT! What harm can come from it? He'll forgive you later, right?

POOF!

Nice work, Lisa.

So Many Deals

Getting a whole lot of my shopping done online today, Jesus. There are so many deals out there!

A "deal" is not a good reason to go into debt, Ann.

But the interest rate on my credit card is very low, plus I earn points for every purchase I make.

The borrower is the lender's slave, Ann, no matter how the lender dresses it up to trick the borrower into thinking otherwise.

Paradise

What is paradise like, Jesus?

Well, one of the first things people notice is that there's no advertising.

So then I suppose hell is filled with advertising?

Personal injury attorneys, used car dealers, ab machines, get-rich-quick schemes. All the worst, 24/7, and at super-high volume...Oh, plus fire.

© Radio Free Babylon

Stirs Their Faith

I hate hospital visitations, Jesus. I'm always at a loss for words in those situations.

I'd prefer it that way, Joe. Trite words are no comfort at all to the sick and their families.

But people are looking to me for comfort, Jesus. They want me to be the one who shows up and stirs their faith.

Then they're looking to the wrong guy.

Just show up, Joe. I'll take it from there.

© Radio Free Babylon

Faceprint

There were two sets of foot-prints in the sand, and every once in a while, there'd be this one faceprint.

And the remainders of a campfire where I stopped to grill you some fish before we set off on our path again.

So, what's the deal?

You were supposed to carry me, like the poem says.

Touching, that poem.

But sometimes what you need is a nice solid faceplant before we can keep walking.

© Radio Free Babylon

One Ugly Garden

I've got so much to do today, Son of Man. Gonna sow some doubt and fear. Plant a bunch of anxiety. Fertilize a good crop of discord.

That's going to be one ugly garden, Satan.

Oh, it's coming along quite nicely.

Quite nicely indeed!

You're forgetting one thing.

I control the rain.

Precarious

The world is so uncertain these days, Jesus.

Everything seems so precarious.

Lisa, you're doing it again.

I know, I know. I'm sorry.

I'll try not to worry so much.

It's as easy as plucking two letters from "precarious."

Then you can see everything as precious instead.

In the Meantime

I hope this doesn't sound ungrateful, Jesus, but I look forward to that sweet relief, to the end of this struggle and trial.

I know, Ann, and I look forward to greeting you, but in the meantime...

I know, I know. Nose to the grindstone, shoulder to the wheel, hand to the plough.

All of that, yes. But more importantly, Ann, heart to God, hand to man.

SATAN

Occupation: Accuser of the Brethren
Age: Older Than Dirt
Marital Status: It's Complicated

He goes about as a roaring lion, seeking whom he may devour. Other times he goes about as a purring kitten, seeking whose ankles he might snuggle up against. He's subtle, smooth, sexy and smart, and he wants to get to know you better. He doesn't think you need to be spending so much time with this silly Nazarene carpenter, who after all is the cause of every war, hardship and atrocity. How could a God who claims to be love send hurricanes and earthquakes? Why is there murder and evil in this world? Why do children suffer and men fight? What kind of a god allows this?

Fine, you want to walk the path of the Galilean; that grungy, backwoods guy born within the stench of donkey and cattle dung? Then Satan will collect some rocks. Some are obvious; big boulders standing in your way. Others he just pelts at you from the bushes, giving you bruises and little scars to remember him by. Still others are tiny pebbles that he slips in your shoes when you're not looking, and it makes it harder for you to walk.

And if you pay him attention, he delights in it. "Keep your eyes on me, little human," he says, "and off the pierced one. What has he ever done for you anyway? Aren't you sad, wretched and miserable? Didn't he promise you life, and in abundance? Look at you! You've been abandoned! Humility is stupid! Pride is what you need!"

Resist, James said, and he gives up.

Seasons & Special Events

THE NEW YEAR

Resolutions

Starting today, J-Man, I'm gonna quit drinking, quit smoking, eat better, work out, spend quality time with Lisa and devote more time to you.

And likely in that order, Carl. That's certainly a full slate of resolutions. And by this time next week, you'll be sorely disappointed in yourself.

That's crazy talk, Jeez! I can do this! I can feel it! This is my year! I'm turning over a new leaf!

You've set yourself an *entire tree* to turn over, son. Start slow. Let's work on the *devoting more time to me* thing. We'll focus on your flabby gut later.

Fresh Start

New year, new me, Jesus.

Let every day be a fresh start, Ann.

In that case, maybe I'll start tomorrow.

And that's what you'll be saying next week.

FRIDAY THE THIRTEENTH

Friday the Thirteenth

It's all I could do to get out of bed and meet you here this morning, Jesus. Friday the thirteenth just terrifies me.

Nonsense. Shake off this irrational fear, Ann. Today is just a day. That is all it is. Nothing in the stars. Nothing in the cards.

And what if something bad happens to me today? What am I to consider that other than bad luck?

Consider it life. Or if it makes you feel better, imagine that the entire cosmos was out to get you today because you are so important.

© Radio Free Babylon

VALENTINE'S DAY

Valentine's Day

I told Lisa, "It's a contrived holiday designed by marketers to sell jewelry, cards, chocolate, flowers and lingerie. You don't have to get me anything."

That's very gracious of you, Carl, but I think you know that Valentine's Day means something to your wife, whether or not it does to you.

Oh, I know. I'm headed over to Victoria's Secret at lunch to grab her something sexy.

Make sure the card reads, *"Roses are red, violets are blue, when I picked this out, I was thinking about you... wearing it for me."*

What Should Matter

Roses are red, violets are blue, even though I hate this holiday, here's some flowers, a card and some chocolates, Lisa.

I thought you looked at Valentine's Day as just a money-grab by the floral industry, Carl.

And the candy makers, greeting-card jerks, jewelry stores...But **you** don't see it that way, and that's what should matter to me.

Wait...who swapped Carl with a guy who's starting to get it?

FIRST DAY OF SPRING

Gotta Love Springtime

Well, spring is here, Jesus! People spreadin' fertilizer on their lawns. Before you know it, 'ol Carl will be up to his knees in yards to mow.

That's great, Carl. Gotta love springtime. Signs of life all about.

Yessir! The ladies shedding their winter coats, bare feet and sun-browned legs soon to follow! *Mmmm! Love me some spring!*

Your appreciation for creation has been noted.

Repeatedly.

RESURRECTION SUNDAY

Happy Easter

Well, if it isn't Mister Sunshine, back from the grave.

Sleep well, Son of Man?

And a Happy Easter to you too, Satan.

Man, if looks could kill...

Oh, wait. You already tried that.

INDEPENDENCE DAY

As Empires Go

Two hundred–plus years of awesomeness! Happy Birthday to the last best hope of man on earth.

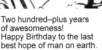

As empires go, that's very young, Kevin.

Like, just out of diapers.

Then imagine how awesome we'll be when we're ready for college!

Not everyone goes to college.

Try to get through the awkward middle school years first.

THE OLYMPIC SPIRIT

That Olympic Spirit

I love that the world can set aside its differences for a couple of weeks and just share that Olympic spirit.

Though I keep hearing how obsessed everyone is over the fact that China has more gold medals than your country.

But we have more medals than them overall! And besides, they snatch babies from their cribs to turn them into drugged robot athletes!

Ah, the spirit of the games.

© Radio Free Babylon

HALLOWEEN

Halloween Candy

All this Halloween candy sitting in my kitchen is not helping the ol' waistline.

It's not the candy sitting in the kitchen that's hurting your waistline, it's the candy you stuff into your fat face. Show some *discipline*, Carl!

Maybe I should take those pills that make you less hungry. How'd you ever go forty days in the desert without any food, Jesus?

After the first thirty days, it's no big deal. But when Satan showed up with those Reese's, I will admit it was tough to hold out.

THANKSGIVING

Homeless Shelter

I signed up to help serve the big Thanksgiving meal down at the homeless shelter again, Jesus. It's so humbling to be there.

Just as humbling, Lisa, for the homeless guys being served by rich white ladies making pitying eyes and small talk.

Jesus, we do it because we care. How else am I going to look? What else am I going to talk about?

Keep in mind while you're there, Lisa, that there's no difference between your Xanax prescription and a bottle of Mad Dog 20/20.

CHRISTMAS

Frosty the Snowman

Frosty the Snowman was a jolly, happy soul.

Frosty the Snowman was no such thing. He was made of snow, Lisa. Then he melted.

No, Jesus! He was alive as he could be! And the children say he could laugh and play just the same as you and me!

But he waved goodbye saying, "Don't you cry, I'll be back again some day," right, Lisa? Wow...wonder where he got *that* line.

© Radio Free Babylon

Pressure to Spend

Every year we talk about the "true meaning of Christmas," Jesus, but I think we're only paying lip service.

It's not easy in this society to cut through the marketing, the hype and the pressure to spend money, Ann.

Tell me about it! Cars, jewelry, toys; every other commercial is another attempt to guilt me into spending.

Resist the devil and he will flee from you, Ann. Also, record your shows and fast forward past his commercials.

Merry Christmas Anyway

We know that shepherds were in the fields at night when you were born, Jesus (Luke 2:7-8). But shepherds aren't in the fields overnight in December!

Oh, no. Here we go.

So the origin of the date, the customs surrounding it, was all a compromise by church leaders to convert pagans, Jesus!

Try to have a Merry Christmas anyway, Kevin.

END OF YEAR

Top Ten Lists

It's that time of year when we all make our top ten lists, Jesus. So, let's hear one from you. Give us your top ten most important events of the year.

Well, number ten would have to be when this little girl in the rural reaches of Jilin Province in China gave her last apple to a very hungry old woman.

Yeah—that's not really how this works, Jesus. You're supposed to pick world news stories or maybe a celebrity screw-up.

You've got your important events, Kevin, I've got mine. Number nine: a single mother of three in Mexico adopted the daughter of her dying neighbor.

Conversations About Coffee with Jesus

offee with Jesus began as an online comic, and like so many things online, it spread by social media. One of the most interesting aspects of social media is that it converts what might otherwise be a private, isolated experience into a conversation. In that spirit, here are some questions that can guide you and your friends in conversations about *Coffee with Jesus*.

1. Wilkie writes, "The notion of Jesus sitting down for a cup of coffee with a bunch of very certain and opinionated people struck me as humorous" (p. 13). What topics are you "very certain and opinionated" about? What do you think Jesus would tease *you* about?

2. "How dare you put words in the mouth of Jesus that he never spoke!" (p. 13 note). The author was accused of this regularly in the early days of the strip. Is that a fair critique? What are the pros and cons of doing so?

3. Is there anything in *Coffee with Jesus* that you don't think the real-life Jesus would say? Explain.

4. Which of the regular characters do you most closely identify with? Which are particularly hard for you to relate to? Why?

5. Satan is often depicted in art, literature and music. How does the depiction of Satan in *Coffee with Jesus* compare with other cultural depictions you've seen? What, in your mind, does *Coffee with Jesus* get right about Satan?

6. Does having Jesus pictured in every strip make it easier or harder for you to imagine your own conversations with him? Explain.

7. "Coffee Jesus" seems friendly, but he also regularly asserts his divine authority. Are you more comfortable with friendly Jesus or Jesus the authority figure? Why?

8. In the strip "About to Say" (p. 19), Jesus predicts that someday Lisa will be able to anticipate

his words to her. What helps you anticipate what God might say to you in a given situation?

9. In the strip "Be Still" (p. 30), Lisa seems to be having an amazing experience with Jesus, even without words (or even *because* there are no words). What do you think is going on in their interaction?

10. Jesus seems to prefer flawed friends to perfect ones. (See the strip "Flawed, Sorry" on p. 30, for example.) Why do you think that is? How does that compare to your perception of Jesus?

11. Jesus often challenges the characters to learn, change, mature, grow up. Which of them is most likely to, do you think? Why? Where do you yourself fall on that spectrum?

12. Some people think comic strips are inherently too juvenile or shallow to learn anything significant from. How would you respond to those people? Explain.

13. Are some issues too serious for humor? What topics do you think should have been left out of *Coffee with Jesus*? Why?

14. The word *imagination* comes up often in the strip. What role do you think the imagination has in living as a Christian?

15. If you had to propose a new "regular" for the strip, who would they be (name, background, personal issues)? What kind of person would make an interesting and funny addition to the cast of characters of "Coffee with Jesus"?

16. "Coffee Jesus" isn't intended to be a fictional character but an accurate portrait. What have you learned about the real Jesus from reading *Coffee with Jesus*?

One of the many goals of Radio Free Babylon is to make people laugh and think—not always in that order and not always simultaneously. This book has hopefully done both of those for you.

We have other plans and means (some of them realized, others still in the planning stages) for continuing to reach people where they live, leaving them scratching their heads or chuckling. Or both. Learn more at

RadioFreeBabylon.com

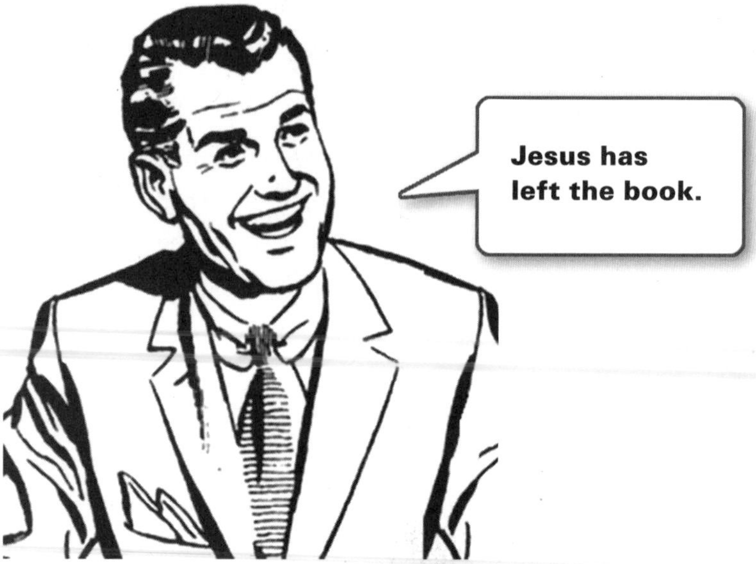
Jesus has
left the book.

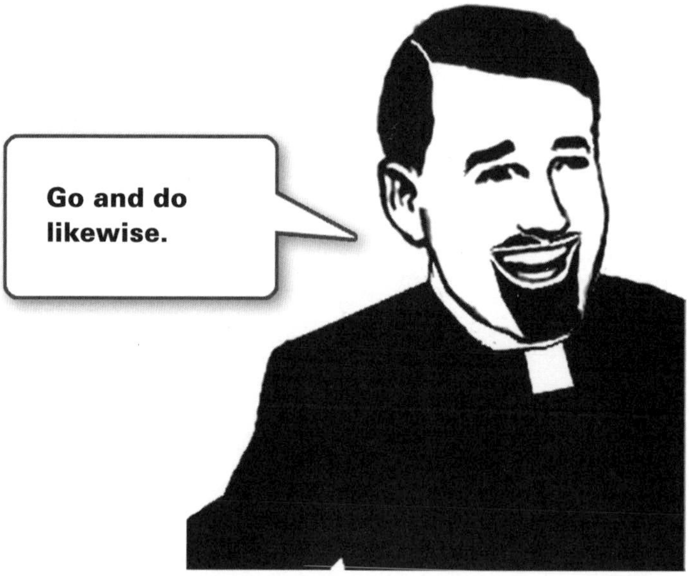
Go and do
likewise.